2 to
IN AUSTRALIA

THE ITINERARY PLANNER

JOHN GOTTBERG

John Muir Publications
Santa Fe, New Mexico

In Fond Memory of the Blue Minx

This book would not have been possible without the assistance of the Australian Tourist Commission, the various state and territory tourist commissions, and the following individuals: Linda Carlock, Rick Steves, Cesare Cataldo, Tamese Gribble, Peggy Bendel, Elaine Kleckner, Patrick J. O'Reilly, Gina Dodd, John Greenslade, Sue Brennan, Sara Longwood, Don Knapp, Amanda Struthers, Scott Thornton, Bob Schatz, Julie and Kevin Keir, Deb and Greg Derwin, Linda and Alan Mulley, Margaret and John Bee.

John Muir Publications, P.O. Box 613, Santa Fe, NM 87504

ISSN 1062-4333
ISBN 1-56261-112-7

Distributed to the book trade by
W.W. Norton & Company, Inc.
New York, New York

Design   Mary Shapiro
Maps   Jim Wood
Cover Photo   Leo de Wys, Inc. / Steve Vidler
Typography   Richard Harris
Printer   Banta Company

CONTENTS

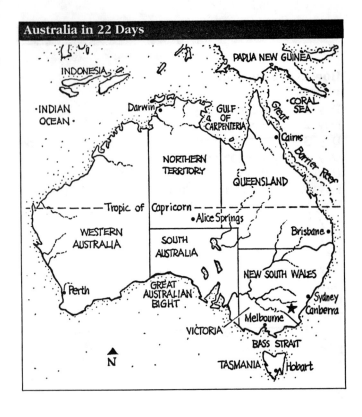

Australia in 22 Days

G'day! In your hands is your fair dinkum, pocket-sized Aussie tour guide. It's designed for independent-minded blokes and birds who like the freedom and flexibility of going walkabout their own way but who appreciate the efficiency that an organized tour offers.

2 to 22 Days in Australia doesn't pretend to take you around the entire continent of "Oz" in three weeks. That would be like trying to see the whole United States in 22 days. It's a fair comparison: Australia is almost identical in size to the 48 contiguous states.

What I have tried to do in this itinerary is to provide a sampling of Australia's most fascinating features—from the great cities of Sydney and Melbourne, to predictable (and worthwhile!) tourist stops such as the Great Barrier Reef and Ayers Rock, to less-known sites like reconstructed gold rush towns and an island of nesting penguins—and suggest how to appreciate them most thoroughly while getting the maximum value for your travel dollar.

Because Australia is so vast, in order to see as much as possible within a three-week itinerary, you should rely on domestic airlines to cover large chunks of land between major attractions. Most of Australia's 16 million people live along the relatively fertile southeast coast, an area well equipped with good roads and visitor facilities. The same is not true of the outback. To get to the dry Centre from any direction, you are faced with a journey of many hundreds of miles across bleak, foreboding terrain. It is probably not a good idea to drive yourself there. Air travel, while no bargain, can save considerable time and worry. With extra time, much of the trip can be done by rental car or (more cheaply and reliably but with somewhat less freedom) by train and bus.

The trip outlined in this book begins in Sydney and concludes in Brisbane. International flights also serve Melbourne and Cairns, allowing you to start and end in any of these gateway cities. I suggest that you leave home on Friday night, arriving in Sydney on Sunday

morning to begin your adventure. This will make connections easier later in the trip. (There are only three Qantas
flights a week from Brisbane to the U.S. West Coast.)

I like to compare any travel plan to a childhood
Erector set. The itinerary should provide a framework for
travel but should not restrict the wanderer from indulging
personal interests or whims. Take this itinerary and cus-
tomize it to your own needs and wants. Make changes.
Scribble in the margins. Cross things out; add new ones.
Spend extra time in one place if it intrigues you; skip
another if you find it boring. If there are things you'd like
to do in Australia that I haven't listed in this book—by all
means, do them.

Each chapter is modular in itself and can be included
as part of whatever itinerary you may want to develop.
The 22 days are organized around the same features
(though not always in this order):

1. An **Introductory Overview** of the day.

2. An hour-by-hour **Suggested Schedule** for the day.

3. A list of **Sightseeing Highlights** (rated: ▲▲▲ Don't
miss; ▲▲ Try hard to see; ▲ Worthwhile if you can make
it).

4. **Orientation** and an easy-to-read **map** of the area.

5. **Transportation** tips and instructions.

6. **Accommodations and Dining:** How and where to
find the best places in your price range, including
addresses, phone numbers, and my favorites.

7. **Itinerary options** for those travelers with more or
less than the suggested time or with particular interests. At
the back of the book, I've included some optional tour
extensions, which expand on the main itinerary.

In deciding when and where to launch your trip, consider holiday and event schedules and seasonal weather
trends. January through March are the rainiest months
along the northern Barrier Reef, for example, while June
through September give the Snowy Mountains their name.
Spring (October to mid-December) and autumn (mid-
March through May) are the best months to cover all cor-
ners of this schedule.

Paperwork

To travel to Australia, you will need a valid passport and a tourist visa. Your tourist visa will cost you nothing except the price of a passport-sized photograph and a self-addressed, stamped (and registered) envelope. Your travel agent can handle everything for you. Allow three weeks for processing. A tourist visa to Australia is typically good for up to six months, with multiple entries allowed for five years or the life of the passport. The tourist visa does prohibit you from working, seeking employment, or taking a major course of study while you are in Australia. These require separate visas that must be obtained from outside the country.

Australian consular offices in the United States are located at:

1601 Massachusetts Avenue N.W., Washington, D.C. 20036 (tel. 202/797-3222)

630 Fifth Avenue, Suite 420, New York, NY 10111 (tel. 212/245-4000)

Quaker Tower, 321 N. Clark Street, Suite 2930, Chicago, IL 60610 (tel. 312/645-9440)

1990 Post Oak Boulevard, Suite 800, Houston, TX 77056 (tel. 713/629-9131)

611 N. Larchmont Boulevard, Los Angeles, CA 90004 (tel. 213/469-4300)

1 Bush Street, 7th Floor, San Francisco, CA 94104 (tel. 415/362-6160)

1000 Bishop Street, Penthouse, Honolulu, HI 96813 (tel. 808/524-5050)

Offices in Canada are located at:

50 O'Connor Street, Suite 710, Ottawa, Ontario K1P 6L2 (tel. 613/236-0841)

Suite 314, 175 Bloor Street E., Toronto, Ontario M4W 3R8 (tel. 416/323-1155)

World Trade Centre, 999 Canada Place, Suite 602, Vancouver, B.C. V6C 3E1 (tel. 604/684-1177)

Cost Considerations

Prices in Australian dollars for transportation, accommodations, food, and so forth, are roughly what you might expect to pay in the United States. The good news is that the Australian dollar is worth about 76 U.S. cents at this writing (May 1993), which means that when you're paying A$50 for a hotel room, you're actually only paying US$38. The same goes for restaurants, where you can pay A$14 for an excellent four-course dinner: in U.S. dollars, you're actually only paying around $11.

The prices estimated and quoted in this book are based on two people traveling together and sharing hotel rooms. If you're traveling alone, you can expect to spend somewhat more. If you're traveling with a larger group, it will cost you a bit less, especially when it comes to hotel rooms and taxi fares. The cost of meals and public transportation won't change much.

Excluding costs of airfares to and from Australia—about US$900 to US$1,500 from the U.S. West Coast—budget travelers can do this 22-day trip for around US$1,500. The budget traveler will stay in hostel-style lodging for A$20 a night or less, travel by bus or train between Sydney and Melbourne, and spend A$444 to fly the Melbourne-Alice Springs-Ayers Rock-Cairns-Brisbane legs of the trip. If it's not important to keep to the 22-day itinerary limit, you can buy a bus pass in lieu of the airfares—although your additional outlay for meals and accommodations will minimize the actual savings.

This trip is ideally suited and designed for the traveler with a little more money in his or her pocket—say, US$3,000 for the three-week journey, not including getting there. If you are this middle-ground tourist, you'll spend an average of A$40 a night (each) for a shared hotel room with private facilities, rent a car for the Sydney-Canberra-Melbourne highway leg, purchase an air pass, and book the occasional tour, like a cruise to the outer Barrier Reef.

The traveler who likes to go everywhere in style, to stay at the best hotels and eat at the best restaurants, will also find this itinerary appropriate. You can do this within a budget of US$5,000 per person, splitting the cost of A$200-a-night hotel rooms, renting a car wherever you want, traveling on an air pass, and booking numerous side tours and cruises during your visit.

The Australian dollar, by the way, is hard to find in paper these days. It's been replaced in everyday use by an A$1 gold-colored coin, leaping kangaroos on the flip side of Queen Elizabeth's portrait. Other coins are the heavy, 12-sided 50-cent piece, the 20-cent piece (slightly larger than an American quarter), the 10-cent piece (similar in size to a dime), the 5-cent piece (about like a Canadian 5-center), the 2-cent piece (copper, bigger than a penny) and the 1-cent penny (much like ours). Paper money, from the lime-green A$2 note to the blue-gray A$100, grows in size and changes color as denominations increase. (In between are $5, $10, $20, and $50 notes.)

It is safest to carry your U.S. dollars in the form of traveler's checks, which you can exchange at city banks 9:30 a.m. to 4:00 p.m. Monday through Thursday and 9:30 a.m. to 5:00 p.m. Friday, and at airport currency counters or major hotel desks anytime.

When to Go

Australia's big tourist season is during the school holidays, which fall in the middle of summer, appropriately—December, January, and into February. This is the warmest time of year Down Under, but for four very good reasons, this is NOT a time of year when I would recommend going to Australia:

1. This is when the Australians are on vacation. You'll find most attractions as well as accommodations heavily booked, and there's a lot of competition to get hold of rental cars, which tends to drive prices up a bit.

2. This is the rainy season in north Queensland; indeed, it's sometimes the cyclone season. Torrents of rain fall in the northern Barrier Reef (Cairns-Townsville) area, especially from January to March. Don't go without your brolly (umbrella).

3. Blowflies—some call them the Australian national bird—are vicious any time in the outback but especially under the hot summer sun.

4. Perhaps most of all, December through March are classified as "high season" by international airlines, which jack up their fares 35 to 50 percent during this period.

You can add US$200 to US$400 to your round-trip airfare if you insist on traveling at this time.

June, July, and August—the North American summer but the Australian winter—are superb in the tropics and subtropics, but the farther south you go, the less pleasant you're likely to find the weather. Melbourne, for example, whose climate is comparable to San Francisco's, can easily have four seasons in a day. What's more, as you travel through Canberra into the Snowy Mountains, you're almost guaranteed to run into snow, and that may cause the closure of some roads.

In my estimation, the ideal times for travel in Australia are autumn (mid-March through May) and spring (September to November). On average, the climate is the best at that time in all parts of the country, and you won't be fighting for rooms like you might be during the peak summer season.

What to Bring
As little as possible. Traveling light frees you from the trials of vagabondage to enjoy your journey more thoroughly. Unless you're in Oz in the winter or are prone to straying into higher elevations, you shouldn't need anything warmer than a sweater and possibly a rain jacket. Cairns, in far north Queensland, is at the same latitude south as Guatemala is north, and it's equally as tropical. The southernmost point on the Australian continent, near Melbourne, if flipped across the equator, would be no farther north than Washington, D.C., or Lake Tahoe.

Tend toward lighter clothes, wash-and-wear items that you can wash in your hotel room and dry overnight. I take what I wear and two more sets of everything. Some say I overpack. Australia is a very informal country, and unless you plan to do business on Collins Street in Melbourne (the only city in Australia where a coat and tie are almost a prerequisite), you'll be fine in any situation with a long-sleeved shirt and slacks or a plain top and wraparound skirt.

If you're going to use them, bring a camera and lenses (only as many as necessary). Buy your film in Australia.

You'll want sunglasses for the beaches and the desert; if you get to the outback and discover you need a wide-brimmed hat with character, choose one there. A good pair of walking shoes is essential. Of course, one thing you should never travel without is a sense of humor.

Flying to Australia

The cheapest fares from North America are from the West Coast gateway cities of Los Angeles, San Francisco, and Vancouver (Canada). It is occasionally possible to find cut-rate or charter tickets for as little as US$650 round-trip. During the April-through-November "low season," you should plan on spending US$900, perhaps up to US$1,100, for an APEX (advance purchase excursion) fare. In December, Australia's "high season," a round-trip APEX fare can run up to US$1,500. October-November and January-February are the "shoulder seasons," with in-between fares.

Most Trans-Pacific flights leave the West Coast between 8:00 p.m. and 11:00 p.m., arriving in Sydney a day and a half later (after crossing the International Date Line) some-time between 6:00 a.m. and 9:00 a.m. Qantas, the Australian national flag carrier, flies daily from both San Francisco and Los Angeles, often with stopovers in Honolulu, Fiji, and/or Tahiti. Nightly service is also offered by Air New Zealand from Los Angeles to Auckland and Sydney via Tahiti or Honolulu and/or Fiji; by United Airlines from Los Angeles to Sydney, nonstop or via Honolulu; by American Airlines from Los Angeles via Honolulu; and by Continental Airlines from San Francisco and Los Angeles. Canadian Pacific Airlines flies twice week-ly from Vancouver to Sydney via Honolulu and/or Fiji, while UTA French Airlines has weekly services from Los Angeles to Sydney via Tahiti, Auckland, and New Caledonia.

Flights originating from the U.S. East Coast are routed through either of the California cities. It's also possible to connect in Great Britain or Europe with Australia-bound flights of Qantas, British Airways, Lufthansa, KLM Dutch Airlines, Air India, Cathay Pacific, Singapore Airlines, and others.

Sydney is 18 hours ahead of the U.S. West Coast, 15
hours ahead of New York and the East Coast. When you
travel west across the Pacific, you're crossing the
International Date Line, so you lose a day. Not to worry, the
Aussies would say. She'll be right. You'll pick up that day
coming home again.

Of course, if you keep moving west, you won't pick up
that day. That's something to consider: for US$2,500, roughly
twice the amount of your round-trip ticket, you could fly
around the world. For US$2,000, you could invest in a circle-
Pacific fare and take in Asia. Read more about those options
in *Asia Through the Back Door* (Santa Fe, N.M.: John Muir
Publications, 1993) by Rick Steves, Bob Effertz, and me.

Getting Around in Australia

As I mentioned earlier within the context of this three-week
itinerary, it is most efficient to fly across large chunks of otherwise tedious territory. The cost-wise way to do this is
through discount airfares.

Ansett Airlines' "Visit Australia Pass" and Australian
Airlines' "Australian Explorer Pass" each can save the traveler
30 to 40 percent off standard coach fares, depending upon
distance or sectors traveled. The only requirements are that
travelers be nonresidents of Australia and be booked in "B"
(economy) class. Make arrangements (and flight reservations) through your travel agent before you leave home or at
the North American offices of these airlines.

The flight segments recommended in this itinerary—
Melbourne–Alice Springs–Ayers Rock–Cairns–Brisbane, some
5,100 km—run A$867 (US$658) at full excursion fare, but
A$600 (US$456) with an air pass.

The Australian Explorer Pass is offered in conjunction
with Qantas, which recently purchased Australian Airlines,
and thus is the recommended pass if you're flying to
Australia aboard Qantas.

Two other transportation pass options may interest budget travelers—bus and train. Some motor coach firms with
extensive national routes offer passes for unlimited travel
within their city-to-city express systems. Australia Coachlines,
which operates Australia's three national bus companies—

Greyhound, Pioneer, and Bus Australia—offers passes for unlimited travel within city-to-city express systems. Options vary from seven days travel in one month (US$251) to 21 days in two months (US$614) or 60 days in three months (US$1,110). Some passes offer half-price sightseeing tours for passholders, and discount motel packages are also available in concert with the coach passes. For information, contact **SoPac Travel Marketing** with a toll-free U.S. number: 800/551-2012.

Railways of Australia have an "Austrailpass" valid for unlimited first-class or economy travel on its route system. The minimum duration is 14 days (US$580 first-class, US$348 economy); one month is US$548 economy, three months cost US$900 economy. There are also passes to travel any eight days in a 60-day period (US$424 first-class, US$256 economy) or any 15 days in a 90-day period (US$600 first-class, US$380 economy). There's an additional charge for overnight berths. All rail passes (good up to 90 days) must be purchased before you travel to Australia, though a seven-day extension is available in Australia.

The rail system in Australia has its limits: the only way to travel from Alice Springs to Cairns is on a bus or via Sydney. So Greyhound and Railways of Australia now jointly offer a "Kangaroo Road 'n Rail Pass" offering combined bus and train travel for 14 to 28 days. Economy fares are US$524 for two weeks, US$920 for four weeks. From North America, contact ATS Tours, which represents Rail Australia, toll-free at 800/423-2880.

My major objection to travel by train or bus is that they carry you only from urban area to urban area. You don't see rural Australia except through smoked windows. Buses and trains pass through an area only two or three times daily; if you want to disembark and take a closer look at something interesting, you're going to have a long wait before the next coach shoots through. You wouldn't even get to the exquisite Victorian gold town of Beechworth; the mainline buses don't go there. And how could you possibly do a wine-tasting tour of Australia's great vineyard districts by bus or train?

Renting a Car and Driving

The best way to see southeastern Australia is to drive your own vehicle. A car allows you much more freedom in your travels, plus an opportunity to get in touch with the "real" Australia. Part of this 22-day tour is geared for the car traveler. If two of you, or better yet, four are traveling together, you'll share the costs of the vehicle and really cut your expenses.

To rent a car in Australia, you must be over 21 years old, preferably have a major credit card, and definitely have a valid driver's license. It is not necessary for you to have an international driver's license. A valid license from any state or Canadian province is quite sufficient.

All major airports have a handful of rental agencies: many are also located in central city areas near major hotels. In Sydney, check the rental agencies on William Street between downtown and Kings Cross. While Hertz and Avis are the old standbys, you'll probably get a better rate from Thrifty or from any number of smaller, locally owned firms.

Plan on an outlay of A$45 to A$75 a day (about US$34 to US$57), including limited kilometers. Petrol (gas), in New South Wales and Victoria priced at 50 to 55 Australian cents a liter (US$1.39 to US$1.65 a gallon), will be your only other major driving expense. (The cost of petrol is slightly cheaper in South Australia and southeastern Queensland, a bit higher in Tasmania and Western Australia.)

Remember that Australia, like most nations of the world, employs the metric system of measurement. There are roughly 3.8 liters to 1 U.S. gallon. Eight kilometers equal about 5 miles.

Your major adjustment driving in Australia rather than North America is that you will be driving a right-hand drive car on the left-hand side of the road. This is not as difficult as you might at first imagine. Everything is simply reversed. Just remember to keep the center line next to the steering wheel, just as you would back home. (But in Australia it's on your right, not on your left.) Your major difficulty may be in turning. Be sure to stay in the left-hand lane: avoid turning across traffic to the right side of the road.

In the cities, you don't need a car and shouldn't use one. It's not worth the frustration, between rush hour traffic, parking hassles, and confusing local laws. (Downtown Melbourne, for instance, requires drivers to pull all the way to the left of an intersection and wait for traffic to clear before turning right.) Inner city public transportation is very good. Buses, Sydney subways, and Melbourne trams are all excellent. Taxis are moderately priced. Turn your car in on arrival in a new city and save yourself many headaches.

"Petrol" isn't the only new word you'll have to learn for driving Down Under. Your car does not have a trunk and a hood; it has a boot and a bonnet. The windshield is known as the windscreen. You don't pass other vehicles, you overtake them. Roads aren't paved; they're sealed, or covered with bitumen. In cities, pavement is what you find across the kerb (curb) on the footpath (sidewalk).

The only roads in Australia that are really in good condition are the main highways—particularly the Sydney-to-Melbourne Hume Highway, a four-lane thoroughfare. Many other roads are in less than optimum shape, sealed but with no shoulders and with lots of ruts and potholes.

Those signs warning Next 10 Km of kangaroos or other Aussie animals should be more than curiosities, especially to night drivers. You won't often see wild animals in the daytime, but please drive carefully after dark.

Where to Stay
Australia has a real choice here, with accommodations of all standards at all price levels. I rate budget accommodations as those costing A$25 and less a night; economy, A$25 to A$75; moderate, A$75 to A$150; and deluxe, over A$150. There are a number of categories to consider.

Hotels run the full gamut from the internationally ranked Regent of Sydney all the way down to the corner pub with a few basic rooms in the attic. Deluxe to economy.

Private hotels are not licensed to sell liquor and therefore are usually lower in cost. Guest houses are private hotels that provide bed and breakfast, often (but not always) included in the tariff. Moderate and economy.

Self-catering apartments are, in essence, hotel suites with their own cooking facilities and sometimes private laundry facilities. Deluxe and moderate.

Motels in Australia offer much the same as their American counterparts. Moderate and economy.

Hostels may or may not be members of the International Youth Hostel Federation. IYH member hostels are located in cities, towns, and national parks throughout the country. Private "backpackers hostels" with similar price structures are more recent developments in major cities and tourist centers. Budget.

Caravan parks are not only for caravans (what Americans call "trailers"). You can set up a tent or, in many cases, stay in a small housekeeping cabin with a hotplate. Budget.

Farm holidays will place you on a "station" far from the bright city lights, where you can watch the dogs muster the sheep—or help a jackeroo round up his cattle by helicopter. Write: 9 Fletcher Street, Woollahra, Sydney, NSW 2025, for details. Moderate and economy.

What and Where to Eat and Drink

Australia is a very cosmopolitan country. This is especially true in Sydney and Melbourne, which have very large populations of South Europeans, Lebanese, and Asians. Nowhere is their influence felt more strongly than in the variety and quality of reasonably priced cuisine. You can eat well at any meal for under A$15. If you plan to spend A$30 per day per person on food, you're perhaps being a little bit extravagant—or else you're budgeting for an occasional splurge at a classier restaurant.

Though not widely acknowledged, there is an Australian cuisine somewhat more imaginative than the bland British and Irish cooking from which it derived. Aussie "tucker" comprises the likes of occasionally palatable dishes such as kangaroo tail soup, meat pies, "snags" (large sausages), damper (unleavened campfire bread), and Vegemite (a strong-tasting yeast spread); more delectable delicacies such as carpetbagger steak (tenderloin stuffed with Sydney rock oysters), roast lamb in mint sauce, pavlova (a meringue dessert); and superb seafood—yabbies (a small lobster), Moreton Bay bugs (another small crustacean), Tasmanian scallops, and indigenous fish like barramundi, jewfish, and John Dory.

I will typically begin my day in Australia with a light breakfast of fresh fruit—pawpaws (papayas) and mangoes are always in season—and/or pastry with a cup of tea or coffee. Later in the morning I might stop for Devonshire tea, served with fresh scones (with whipped cream and strawberry jam). For lunch, I might pick up some fish and chips or a chicko roll at the takeaway counter of a milk bar (sort of like a 7-11 with a fast-food counter). More often, I'll pause for pub grub. You never really go wrong if you eat in a pub. The price is right— often A$5 to A$8 for a full meal—and you can pick some pretty good meals off the blackboard menu: roast chicken, grilled fish, steak-and-kidney pie, even cook your own T-bone. At dinnertime, I'll often head off to the European or Asian section of town, read the menus posted in the windows, and wander in where I see the locals eating. And I almost always wash it down with a glass of good Aussie beer or wine. Many restaurants acclaim themselves as "BYO": bring your own alcoholic beverage. They may charge a small corkage fee, but their prices are almost always lower than those of licensed restaurants, and it's no great inconvenience to stop by the bottle shop at a nearby pub (pub "public hotel").

Beer is the Australian national drink, and it certainly deserves that distinction. Those who compile such statistics say the Aussies drink more beer per capita—some 30 gallons annually—than anyone but the Bavarians and Belgians. Every state has its own breweries and is stubbornly proud of its local brews. Drink from middies or pots (10-ounce glasses) or from schooners (15 ounces).

Australian wine has become recognized as among the best in the world. The principal growing areas are the

Barossa Valley, focused on Tanunda northeast of
Adelaide; and the Hunter Valley, around Cessnock north
of Sydney. Victoria and Western Australia also have
excellent wineries. Riesling, semillon, chardonnay, and
white burgundy are among the better white wines; in the
reds, consider claret, cabernet sauvignon, shiraz, and
merlot.

Information Sources

This slender tome is not intended to be more than a travel planner used in conjunction with a more complete
guidebook. Lonely Planet's *Australia: A Travel Survival
Kit*, by Tony Wheeler et al., has long been the bible of
shoestring travelers in Australia, and deservedly so. The
book has grown to become a very comprehensive volume of some 400 pages thoroughly covering the entire
continent. It is a book that no traveler, especially no budget traveler, should go without. An option, not as
detailed nationwide but reasonably good in major cities,
is Frommer's *Australia on $40 a Day* by John Godwin.
For middle- and upper-income travelers looking to get
the most quality for their dollar, I highly recommend
Robert W. Bone's *Maverick Guide to Australia* (Gretna,
La.: Pelican). An excellent book for planning your trip
and to keep as a souvenir when your trip is over is Apa
Publications' lavishly illustrated *Insight Guide: Australia.*
You should be able to find any of these books at major
bookshops across North America.

In planning, don't overlook the assistance you can get
from the Australian Tourist Commission and from the
individual state and territory tourist boards. They can
provide an enormous amount of valuable information for
your journey. They also can provide the best highway
maps I've found on Australia and its separate states. It's
all free, and all commissions have offices in North
America.

Australia Tourist Commission

489 Fifth Avenue, 31st floor, New York, NY 10017 (tel. 212/687-6300)

2121 Avenue of the Stars, Suite 1200, Los Angeles, CA 90067 (tel. 310/552-1988)

150 N. Michigan Avenue, Suite 2130, Chicago, IL 60601 (tel. 312/781-5150)

2 Bloor Street W., Suite 1730, Toronto, Ontario M4W 3E2, Canada (tel. 416/925-9575)

Australia Naturally (Victoria and Tasmania)

2121 Avenue of the Stars, Suite 1270, Los Angeles, CA 90067 (tel. 310/553-6352)

New South Wales Tourism Commission

2121 Avenue of the Stars, Suite 450, Los Angeles, CA 90067 (tel. 310/552-9566)

Northern Territory Tourism Commission

2121 Avenue of the Stars, Suite 1230, Los Angeles, CA 90067 (tel. 310/277-7877)

Queensland Tourist and Travel Corporation

1800 Century Park East, Suite 330, Los Angeles, CA 90067 (tel. 310/788-0997)

Tourism South Australia

2121 Avenue of the Stars, Suite 1210, Los Angeles, CA 90067 (tel. 310/552-2821)

Western Australian Tourism Commission

2121 Avenue of the Stars, Suite 1210, Los Angeles, CA 90067 (tel. 310/557-1987)

Other Reading

Nearly all Aussies identify with the outback, the "bush," even if they are (as are most) urban dwellers. To get a feeling for this tradition, I would go back to the short stories and poetry of nineteenth-century writers Henry Lawson and A. B. "Banjo" Paterson. Lawson is more highly acclaimed in Australia, though Paterson's ballads— "Waltzing Matilda" and "The Man from Snowy River"— are better known to Americans.

The best Australian novel in recent years is Colleen McCullough's *The Thorn Birds*. Some North Americans know the miniseries (starring Richard Chamberlain) better than the book. Also outstanding is Thomas Kenneally (*The Chant of Jimmy Blacksmith*). A young Aussie writer who impresses me is Tim Winton (*That Eye, the Sky*).

Good histories are Donald Horne's *The Australian People: Biography of a Nation* and F. R. Crowley's *A New History of Australia.* Robert Hughes's superb *The Fatal Shore* (1987) deals with Australia's convict history and, indirectly, its impact on the modern nation. For a better understanding of aboriginal history and culture, see *Australian Dreaming,* edited by Jennifer Isaacs, or Bruce Chatwin's *The Songlines.* Titles by Michael Morcombe and Eric Worrell are among the best dealing with Australia's rich natural history.

Write Me a Letter
Change affects Australia as it does everywhere in the world. No matter how hard I try to keep this book up to date, there's always going to be something I miss. If this volume helps you enjoy your trip, if it doesn't help you, if you've found things that need more explanation, if you've found things that would add to the enjoyment of other travelers, I would love to hear from you. Please send your trips and recommendations, love mail and hate mail, criticism and corrections, c/o John Muir Publications, P.O. Box 613, Santa Fe, NM 87504. In return for ideas used, I'll send you a free copy of my next edition. Meanwhile, happy travels!

Whenever I mention to an Australian that I'm the author of a book entitled *2 to 22 Days in Australia*, I'm greeted first with a dazed look, then a chuckle. "Oh, you'd be buggered after that one, mate!" they say as they shout me another beer. But the fact remains that most Americans, if they're lucky, have only three weeks of vacation in which to see Australia. So here is my suggested itinerary, which I hope provides the best sampling of the country in a limited period of time. I encourage you to add days for relaxation whenever possible, because the pace of travel—over 4,000 miles in a very short time—can be exhausting. Here is an overview of the 22-day itinerary.

DAY 1 (Sunday) Arrive in Sydney in the morning, get set up in your accommodation, then enjoy an afternoon cruise on beautiful Sydney Harbour. Call it quits right after dinner tonight, cheating jet lag with an early bed-time.

DAY 2 (Monday) The Sydney Explorer bus will escort you to all major city sights for one set fare. Highlights will include the famous Opera House, the Australian Museum, and The Rocks, Sydney's oldest neighborhood. Enjoy an atmospheric dinner at the Argyle Tavern in The Rocks, with bush ballad sing-alongs.

DAY 3 (Tuesday) Exercise your options. I like to start the day at Bondi Beach, then visit the colonial Vaucluse House mansion and wander through the suburbs of Double Bay and Paddington. If it's marsupials you want to see, take the ferry across the harbor to Taronga Park Zoo, and include a visit to Manly, with its famous surf beach and Marineland. History buffs may want to visit Old Sydney Town in Gosford; oenophiles should make a side trip to the Hunter Valley. Spend the night at Kings Cross, where you can play or gape at others playing.

Tour Route

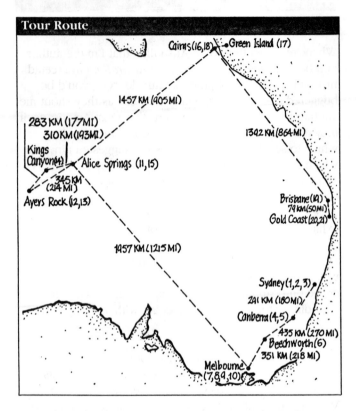

Cairns (16,18) Green Island (17)

1457 KM (905 MI)

283 KM (177MI)
310 KM (193MI)

1302 KM (864 MI)

Kings
Canyon(14) Alice Springs (11,15)

345 KM
(214 MI)

Ayers Rock (12,13)

Brisbane (19)
79 km (50MI)
Gold Coast (20,21)

1957 KM (1215 MI)

Sydney (1,2,3)

281 KM (180MI)

Canberra (4,5)

435 KM (270 MI)
Beechworth (6)
351 KM (218 MI)

Melbourne
(7,8,9,10)

DAY 4 (Wednesday) Pick up your reserved rental car in Sydney early this morning, with plans to leave it in Melbourne in a week. After a stop to see the working sheep farm at Gledswood homestead, continue to historic Berrima for lunch. On arrival in the modern national capital, visit the Canberra Planning Exhibition to understand the design and evolution of the city, then drive to the top of Mount Ainslie for a good overview.

DAY 5 (Thursday) Explore Canberra. Start at the Parliament House, if possible watching the House of Representatives or Senate in session from a public gallery. Take a drive through the Yarralumla area to see the impressive row of national embassies, then lunch at the High Court, inspect the National Gallery, and visit the Australian War Memorial museum.

DAY 6 (Friday) There's a long day of driving ahead, so get an early start. Today's route leads past the alpine resort of Thredbo in the Snowy Mountains and via Corryong, reputed home of poet Banjo Paterson's "Man from Snowy River," to Beechworth, a town straight out of the nineteenth-century gold rush era.

DAY 7 (Saturday) After a morning look at Beechworth, visit the Brown Brothers Winery, one of Australia's finest, and stop in Glenrowan, where Ned Kelly, Australia's most notorious frontier bushranger, made his "last stand." The afternoon's highlight is the Sir Colin McKenzie Wildlife Sanctuary at Healesville, an open-air reserve that is the best of its kind in the world. You'll reach Melbourne in time for dinner.

DAY 8 (Sunday) Explore Melbourne today. Wander through its ethnic neighborhoods, its sophisticated shopping arcades, its highbrow business district. Don't miss the beautiful Victorian Arts Centre or the nation's best botanic gardens. The Old Gaol and the National Museum are worthy stops. But don't overdo the sightseeing. Here in sports-crazy Melbourne, you should soak up some Australian culture with (depending on the season) a visit to a "footie" match, a cricket test, or a horse race.

DAY 9 (Monday) Drive to Ballarat, site of Australia's greatest gold rush and its most famous rebellion. The Sovereign Hill theme park realistically re-creates the town's heyday. The adjacent Gold Museum and the Eureka Exhibition memorialize Eureka Stockade, the nation's 1854 reply to Bunker Hill. Return to Melbourne in the late afternoon.

DAY 10 (Tuesday) Drive east into the Dandenong Ranges, where you can wonder at William Ricketts's unique forest sculptures or search for lyrebirds in Sherbrooke Forest. Proceed to Phillip Island, where fairy penguins parade from the sea at dusk. Then return to Melbourne.

DAY 11 (Wednesday) Drop your car at Melbourne's Tullamarine airport and catch a morning flight to Alice Springs. You'll have all afternoon and evening to explore this outback oasis. Stop by the Old Telegraph Station, the Royal Flying Doctor Service, and the Aboriginal art galleries. Climax your day with something unique: ride a camel down the dry Todd River bed to dinner at a desert winery.

DAY 12 (Thursday) Marvel at the weird geology of the Red Centre as you fly from Alice Springs to Yulara resort village at Ayers Rock, arriving in the early afternoon. Get settled in your lodging and explore the community, then sip champagne as you watch the sun set over the red rock. Turn in early, because tomorrow, if you're energetic, you will . . .

DAY 13 (Friday) . . . climb the Rock. If the world's largest monolith is awesome at sunset, it's even more stunning at dawn. Awaken early to watch the light change its appearance and to beat the heat and flies as you scale the huge red rock so that you, too, can wear a T-shirt declaring, "I Climbed Ayers Rock." Then visit the craft exhibit at the Uluru National Park ranger station and search for ancient petroglyphs in caves around the base of Ayers Rock.

DAY 14 (Saturday) Learn about the Aboriginal culture today. Spend the morning with a native guide who will show you how her people found food, water, shelter, and medicine in this arid landscape. After lunch, board a bus for the 175-mile drive to the Kings Canyon Frontier Lodge.

DAY 15 (Sunday) Explore colorful Kings Canyon, then return to Alice Springs in the evening. If you're not exhausted, enjoy a nightcap at the casino.

DAY 16 (Monday) A travel day, Alice Springs to Cairns. On arrival in Cairns, the humidity will tell you immediately that you are in the tropics. Have a cold beer at an Esplanade pub and watch the fishing and pleasure boats come and go to the Great Barrier Reef. For dinner, order barramundi, a delectable river-run reef cod.

DAY 17 (Tuesday) You'll leave Cairns this morning to spend the day snorkeling or diving on the outer Barrier Reef. This experience should not be missed. More than 200 species of tropical reef fish can be seen swimming through a fantastic undersea "garden" of multicolored coral.

DAY 18 (Wednesday) The scenic Kuranda Railway will take you inland to the edge of the rain-forested Atherton Tableland, climbing steeply above fields of sugarcane to the Barron River Gorge and Barron Falls. You'll reach Kuranda in time to see the famous Tjapukai Aboriginal dance troupe perform. See the wildlife noctarium after lunch and the butterfly sanctuary before returning to Cairns for dinner.

DAY 19 (Thursday) Take an early morning flight south to Brisbane, check into your hotel, then join the "koala cruise" to Lone Pine Koala Sanctuary, Brisbane's No. 1 tourist sight. If you ever wanted a photo of yourself holding one of these seemingly cuddly creatures, here's where to have it taken. The cruise winds its way up the meandering Brisbane River. After a dinner of Moreton Bay bug (it's a crustacean, not an insect), check out the evening offerings at the Queensland Cultural Centre.

DAY 20 (Friday) Take a bus to the Gold Coast, Australia's version of Miami Beach. You've got the entire afternoon on the beach—after all, you need a tan to show off when you get home.

DAY 21 (Saturday) Your final full day on Australian beaches. The Gold Coast's biggest town is called Surfers Paradise; why not decide for yourself if the name really fits? Or you can dive into tourist attractions such as Sea

World, the Currumbin Bird Sanctuary, or the Mudgeeraba Boomerang Factory.

DAY 22 (Sunday) It's been a great three weeks. Board your flight home to the States in Brisbane this evening You'll reach the U.S. West Coast only 1½ hours after leaving Australia, thanks to the International Date Line. The longest day of your life was custom made for savoring those great Australian memories.

ARRIVE IN SYDNEY

Welcome to Australia! This is your first day Down Under, but you have many more to come, so don't exhaust yourself too quickly. You will arrive in Sydney in the morning. After clearing customs and immigration, travel into the city, get set in your hotel, refresh yourself, then spend the afternoon on a leisurely cruise of the beautiful Sydney Harbour.

Suggested Schedule

6:30- 9:30 a.m.	Arrive at Sydney Airport.
7:30-10:30 a.m.	Take a bus into the city.
8:15-11:15 a.m.	Get set up in your accommodation.
12:30 p.m.	Lunch.
2:00 p.m.	Sydney Harbour "Coffee Cruise" from Circular Quay. Or take a ferry to Manly.
5:00 p.m.	Return to hotel.
6:30 p.m.	Dinner in Darlinghurst.
9:00 p.m.	Collapse into bed.

Airport Orientation

Kingsford Smith (Sydney) International Airport is located about 10 km south of the city center on Botany Bay. (Start thinking in metrics as soon as you arrive: 10 kilometers is about 6 miles.) When your plane drops in over the bay, you'll be arriving Down Under at almost the same exact place as Captain James Cook, the first European to visit Australia, in 1770. Unlike Cook, you'll have to clear immigration and customs. Cap'n Jim was fortunate not to have to go through those formalities two centuries ago.

Travelers unlucky enough to arrive at the same time as a half dozen other international flights will disagree, but I've always found the immigration procedures relatively painless here. Hopefully, you'll zoom through quickly, wait a few minutes to pluck your luggage from the baggage carousels, then move straight through customs into the arrival hall.

Change some money into Australian dollars at the airport bank, to the right. The rate here isn't quite as good as you'll find at the banks in the city, but the counters are open to meet all incoming international flights; and if you've followed my suggestion and arrived on a Saturday, you'll need enough cash to get you through the weekend. (At this writing, I was getting A$1.29 to US$1 at the airport, A$1.32 in town. Incidentally, some banks charge as much as A$5 commission for transactions; others assess no commission. Inquire before you exchange.)

At the south end of the arrival hall (farthest from the bank) is the Travellers Information Service desk. Here you can obtain hotel reservations, maps, and information on tourist attractions in Sydney and book a shuttle-bus ticket into town. A bus ticket, which entitles you to be dropped off at most hotels within the City Centre-Kings Cross area, costs A$5. Taxis run about A$18. Turn a cold shoulder on the rental car agents for now: you don't need one in the city. Public transportation is excellent, and you'll save a lot of money, not to mention parking and driving hassles, if you wait to pick up a car until you leave Sydney in three days.

If you haven't yet booked your domestic flight segments, take the escalator upstairs to the departure hall and do it now. Using the Australian Explorer Pass, take Australian Flight 22 from Melbourne to Alice Springs at 7:50 a.m. on Day 11, Flight 56 from Alice Springs to Ayers Rock at 12:20 p.m. on Day 12, Flight 299 from Alice Springs to Cairns at 4:25 p.m. on Day 16, and Flight 6 from Cairns to Brisbane at 6:00 a.m. on Day 19. (Flight schedules change frequently, so consult an airline or travel agent before finalizing arrangements.)

Sydney Orientation
Over 20 percent of all Australians live in metropolitan Sydney. These 3 million lucky people make their homes

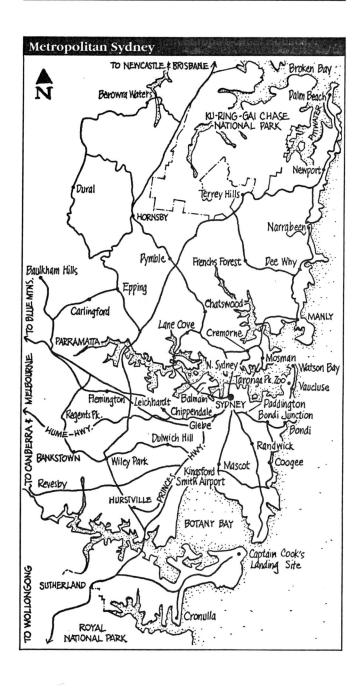

Metropolitan Sydney

TO NEWCASTLE & BRISBANE

Broken Bay

Berowra Waters

Palm Beach

KU-RING-GAI CHASE NATIONAL PARK

Newport

Dural

Terrey Hills

HORNSBY

Narrabeen

Pymble

Frenchs Forest

Dee Why

Baulkham Hills

Epping

Chatswood

Carlingford

Lane Cove

Cremorne

MANLY

PARRAMATTA

N. Sydney

Mosman

Watson Bay

Taronga Pk. Zoo

Vaucluse

Flemington

Leichhardt

Balmain

SYDNEY

Paddington

Regents Pk.

Chippendale

Bondi Junction

Glebe

Bondi

HUME-HWY.

Dulwich Hill

Randwick

BANKSTOWN

Wiley Park

Mascot

Coogee

Revesby

Kingsford Smith Airport

HURSTVILLE

BOTANY BAY

Captain Cook's Landing Site

SUTHERLAND

Cronulla

ROYAL NATIONAL PARK

TO BLUE MTNS.

TO CANBERRA & MELBOURNE

TO WOLLONGONG

in one of the great cities on earth. It has everything they might ask for: a beautiful setting around a long, deep-blue harbor, a rich and varied cultural life, restaurants and hotels to suit all tastes and spending abilities, and activities enough to support a book that could be entitled *2 to 22 Days in Sydney.*

Not only is Sydney Australia's largest city; it was also its first. On January 26, 1788, Captain Arthur Phillip arrived in Port Jackson (Sydney Harbour) with his "First Fleet" of eleven ships. He landed close to the site of the modern Harbour Bridge and established a settlement in the area known today as The Rocks. Nearly three-quarters of his 1,030 passengers were convicts, most of them deported from the British Isles for petty thievery, forgery, and similar trumped-up charges. They became the foundation of the colony and the nation, and it is their success that Australia celebrated in its Bicentennial observance in 1988.

The oldest buildings standing in Sydney today are a legacy of Governor Lachlan Macquarie (1809-1821), who set an egalitarian standard for Australia by ordering the emancipation of deserving convicts to give them a "fair go" alongside free settlers. Yet it wasn't until the twentieth century, first with Commonwealth status ("independence") in 1901 and later with an influx of European immigrants, that the city really boomed.

Sydney's climate is similar to that of Los Angeles—without the smog. The mean summer temperature (December to February) is 78 degrees Fahrenheit; the winter mean (June to August) is 55 degrees. Average annual rainfall is 47.5 inches, with June the rainiest month (5.1 inches) and September the driest (0.6 inch). With such a comfortable climate, Sydneysiders love the outdoors. On most weekends and sunny afternoons you'll find them on their boats in the harbor or spangling the many fine beaches.

Though Sydney sprawls for many miles around the harbor, it's easy to find your way around the central area. Circular Quay, where ferries and cruise boats dock, is your point of orientation. East of the Quay, jutting into the harbor on Bennelong Point, is the Opera House, and immediately south of it the botanic gardens and The Domain. Macquarie Street is the main north-south thoroughfare here. West of the Quay, George and Pitt streets run from The Rocks (at the foot of the Harbour Bridge) through the City Centre to Chinatown and the central railway station. Park Street (becoming William Street) intersects George and Pitt streets at Sydney Town Hall and proceeds east, dissecting Hyde Park and running about a mile to Kings Cross. The Martin Place pedestrian mall, halfway between Park Street and Circular Quay, spans five blocks from George Street to Macquarie Street.

City Transportation

Between the subway/train, the monorail, and the bus and ferry systems, Sydney is extremely well served by all forms of public transportation.

The Sydney Metropolitan Rail System (tel. 214-1067) serves 176 stations in nine lines running west, south, north, and east of Central Station. The City Circle subway line runs continuously from 5:00 a.m. to midnight between Museum, St. James, Circular Quay, Wynyard, Town Hall, and Central stations; the Eastern Suburbs line connects Town Hall with Martin Place, Kings Cross, and on to Bondi Junction. Systemwide maps can be obtained from any visitor information center. Standard fares for short distances are A$1.10. The new TNT Harbourlink monorail (tel. 552-2288) connects city center stations with Darling Harbour at a cost of A$2 per trip.

Buses of the Urban Transit Authority of New South Wales (tel. 954-4422) serve every corner of the metropolis that the trains miss. Fares start at A$1.30. Bus No. 777 operates in the central city area at 10-minute intervals from 9:30 a.m. to 3:30 p.m. Monday through Friday. No. 666 connects Wynyard station with the Art Gallery of New South Wales in The Domain. Tourists are well served by the Sydney Explorer, a bright red double-decker bus that runs an 18-km loop to 22 major attractions for a set fee of A$15. The service operates continuously from 9:30 a.m. to 8:30 p.m. daily at 15- to 17-minute intervals.

The Urban Transit Authority also operates the ferry service from Circular Quay (6-digit tel. 274-738) between 6:00 a.m. and 11:00 p.m. daily. The one-way fare is A$3 west to Hunters Hill and Greenwich, or across the harbor to Mosman, Cremorne, and Neutral Bay. To Manly, near the head of the harbor, it costs A$4 by ferry or A$5 by hydrofoil.

A good option for tourists is the SydneyPass. Priced at A$45 for three days, A$65 for five days, or A$75 for a full week, it offers unlimited travel on Sydney buses and ferries, the Sydney Explorer, the Airport Express bus, and special harbor cruises. Buy it upon arrival at the Travellers Information Service desk at the Sydney airport or directly from most travel suppliers.

Where to Stay
Sydney's best hotels are a boomerang's throw from Circular Quay and The Rocks. **The Regent of Sydney**, 199 George Street (tel. 238-0000), is ranked among the world's elite: it's very expensive but worth every penny, I'm told. Just down the street, and a small step down in price, is the **Old Sydney Parkroyal**, right in The Rocks at 55 George Street (tel. 252-0524). A well-entrenched favorite is the **Sheraton Wentworth**, 61 Phillip Street (tel. 230-0700).

For lower-cost lodging, the best selection is in Kings Cross, Sydney's answer to London's Soho and Paris's Pigalle. There's a lot of bustle and sleaze (some call it "character") here, but no real danger as long as you mind your own business. In the moderate price bracket, check out the **Clairmont Inn**, 5 Ward Avenue (tel. 358-2044), or the **Metro Motor Inn**, 40 Bayswater Road (tel. 356-3511).

For real budget accommodations, look on Victoria Street and Hughes Street, where you'll pay as little as A$10 a night in a dorm (perhaps A$20 a night in a shared double room) at a dozen small private hotels and backpackers' hostels. There's not a lot to choose between in these places; I opt for the inns with TV and rec rooms, not to mention good travelers' bulletin boards. Try the **Travellers Rest**, 156 Victoria Street (tel. 358-4606), or the **Downunder Hostel**, 25 Hughes Street (tel. 358-1433). No hostel in the Cross is a member of the International Youth Hostel Federation; there are IYH hostels farther out at 262 Glebe Point Road, Glebe (tel. 692-8418); 51 Hereford Street, Glebe (tel. 660-5577); and 407 Marrickville Road, Dulwich Hill (tel. 569-0272).

Where to Eat
The best restaurant strip in Sydney, both in terms of price and variety of cuisine, is Oxford Street in Darlinghurst, less than 1 km south of Kings Cross via Darlinghurst Road or Victoria Street. For less than A$15 per person, you can eat well at such diverse ethnic eateries as **Old Saigon**, (Vietnamese, No. 107), **Tin Hong** (Chinese, No. 128), the **Balkan** (Greek, No. 209-215), **Thai Silver Spoon** (No. 203), **Afrilanka** (East African-Sri Lankan, No. 237), or **Borobudur** (Indonesian, No. 263), among many others. Around the corner and down the street are Sydney's best selections for budget watchers: **No Names** (that's what the locals call it; it really doesn't have a name), 2 Chapel Street, a half-block south of Stanley Street off Crown Street, and the **Metro Café**, 26 Burton Street west of Crown. At either, you can get simple but huge pasta-and-salad meals for around A$10. **Laurie's**, opposite Green Park at Victoria and Burton streets, has innovative vegetarian cuisine.

In the Cross, you'll get a tasty if pricey meal at the upscale **Bayswater Brasserie**, 32 Bayswater Road. Other moderate-priced options: **The Astoria**, 7 Darlinghurst Road, for home-style Australian, and **The Last Aussie Fishcaf**, 24 Bayswater Road.

Downtown, you can dine like an affluent tourist at the
Bennelong Restaurant in the Opera House, or in higher
style yet in the revolving restaurants atop **Sydney Tower**
or **Australia Square** (which is round, incidentally). More
popular among locals in a moderate price range are
Johnny Walker's Bistro in Angel Place (near Martin
Place) for steaks; **Machiavelli Ristorante**, 123 Clarence
Street, for Italian; **Capitan Torres**, 73 Liverpool Street, for
tapas and Spanish entrées; **Pancakes on the Rocks**, 10
Hickson Road, for 24-hour munchies; and the **Imperial
Peking Harbourside**, 15 Circular Quay West, for upmar-
ket Chinese food.

If you want to eat like the Asians, visit the **Chinatown
Food Fair**, Dixon and Goulburn streets (third floor), open
from 11:00 a.m. to 11:00 p.m. daily (to 9:00 p.m. Sundays).
You can sate your appetite for under A$5 while choosing
your meal from over a dozen Southeast Asia-style food
stalls. There's a smaller version of same at **Dixon
Gourmet**, Dixon and Little Hay streets. Away from
Sydney's core, two restaurants deserve a special mention.
Doyle's on the Beach, at Watson's Bay near the south
head of the harbor mouth, is so famous for its seafood that
it runs a special shuttle ferry from a dock near Circular
Quay. The **Berowra Waters Inn**, Berowra, is considered
the best of all possible restaurants in Australia. To get
there, you must drive an hour north from the city center to
a jetty, where you are met by a private punt. It's open
Friday to Sunday only, and bookings are required.

Helpful Hints
The **Travel Centre of New South Wales**, 19 Castlereagh
Street in the heart of downtown, provides maps and
brochures and books seats for tours or entertainment
events, 9:00 a.m. to 5:00 p.m. weekdays. **The Rocks
Visitors Centre**, 104 George Street (tel. 247-4972), handles local sightseeing, tours, and other requests from 8:30
a.m. to 5:30 p.m. Monday to Friday and 9:00 a.m. to 5:00
p.m. Saturday.

The **General Post Office** (tel. 230-7033) is on Martin Place at the corner of Pitt Street. It's open 8:15 a.m. to 5:30 p.m. Monday to Friday and 8:30 a.m. to 12:00 noon Saturday. **Banks** are open 9:30 a.m. to 4:00 p.m. Monday through Thursday, 9:30 a.m. to 5:00 p.m. Friday. Most shops are open from 9:00 a.m. to 5:30 p.m. Monday through Wednesday, 9:00 a.m. to 9:00 p.m. Thursday and Friday, 9:00 a.m. to 12:00 noon Saturday.

There's a **U.S. Consulate General** in the T&G Building, Elizabeth and Park streets (tel. 261-9200), and a **Canadian Consulate General** on the 8th floor of the AMP Centre, 50 Bridge Street (tel. 231-6522).

In case of emergencies, dial 000.

AROUND SYDNEY

Today is devoted to exploring the major sights of the city's core. Take the red double-decker bus, the Sydney Explorer (see City Transportation, Day 1), or, better yet, walk.

Suggested Schedule

8:00 a.m.	Breakfast at hotel.
9:00 a.m.	Take the bus or subway or walk to the Opera House, arriving for the guided tour.
10:30 a.m.	Experience the view from Sydney Tower.
11:15 a.m.	Browse through Hyde Park Barracks and the Old Mint.
12:30 p.m.	Picnic lunch in The Domain or Botanic Gardens.
1:30 p.m.	Art Gallery of N.S.W.
3:00 p.m.	Australian Museum.
4:30 p.m.	The Rocks: start a walking tour at the visitor center, but dawdle in the shops and pubs.
7:30 p.m.	Dinner and show at the Argyle Tavern.

Sightseeing Highlights

▲▲▲**Sydney Harbour** (see Day 1)—Life in Sydney centers on the harbor. Thirteen miles (21 km) long from its ocean heads to the mouth of the Paramatta River, with some 160 miles (250 km) of crenelated coastline, the deep blue inlet seems permanently speckled with boats of all sizes and shapes. On sunny weekend afternoons, the colorful jibs of myriad sailboats make the harbor look like a seaborne carnival. The Opera House and Harbour Bridge are its unmistakable landmarks, but there is much more to see: colonial mansions and modern architectural showcases, the skylines of downtown and North Sydney, the laughing face and looming roller coaster of Luna

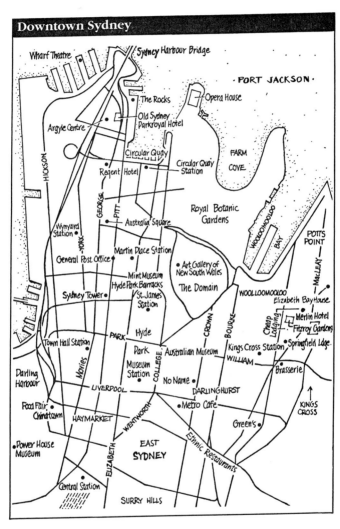

Downtown Sydney

Wharf Theatre · Sydney Harbour Bridge · · PORT JACKSON ·

The Rocks · Opera House

Old Sydney · Parkroyal Hotel

Argyle Centre

HICKSON

Circular Quay · FARM COVE · Circular Quay Station

Regent Hotel

GEORGE · PITT

Royal Botanic Gardens

Australia Square

WOOLLOOMOOLOO · BAY · POTTS POINT

Wynyard Station · YORK

Martin Place Station

General Post Office

MACLEAY

Mint Museum · Art Gallery of New South Wales

Hyde Park Barracks · The Domain · WOOLLOOMOOLOO · Elizabeth Bay House

Sydney Tower · St. James Station · CROWN · BOURKE · Cheap Lodging · Merlin Hotel · Fitzroy Gardens

Town Hall Station · PARK · Hyde Park

Movies

Park Museum Station · COLLEGE · Australian Museum · Kings Cross Station · WILLIAM · Springfield Lodge

Brasserie

No Name · DARLINGHURST

Darling Harbour

LIVERPOOL

Food Fair · Chinatown · HAYMARKET · WENTWORTH · Metro Café · KINGS CROSS

Power House Museum · ELIZABETH · EAST SYDNEY · Ethnic Restaurants · Green's

Central Station · SURRY HILLS

Park, the sandstone turrets of Fort Denison on venerable
Pinchgut Island.

All Harbour cruises leave the city from Circular Quay,
at the foot of Pitt Street. Ferry routes and fares are dis-
cussed in Day 1 under City Transportation. The Urban
Transit Authority's A$45 SydneyPass includes narrated

up- and down-Harbour cruises, shuttles to the Taronga Park Zoo and Manly, and other waterborne options.

There are several cruise operators. I like **Captain Cook Cruises** (tel. 251-5007), with 14 tour options daily from 9:30 a.m. to 7:30 p.m., varying in length from 75 minutes to six hours and in price from A$15 to A$50. A good introductory trip is the Captain Cook Coffee Cruise, leaving No. 6 Jetty every day at 10:00 a.m. and 2:00 p.m. The 2-hour trip includes refreshments.

▲▲▲**Sydney Opera House**, Bennelong Point. One of the most unique buildings on Earth, the Opera House was designed by Danish architect Jorn Utzon, begun in 1959 and opened in 1973. Talk about inflation: its cost was first estimated at A$7 million, but it wound up costing A$102 million! It's really much more than a stage for operas; the complex also contains a concert hall, drama and movie theaters, a recording hall, an exhibition hall, two restaurants, six lounges, a library and archives, and various rehearsal studios, dressing rooms, and administrative offices, all under the distinctive sail-like roofs. Sixty-minute guided tours are conducted daily (except Good Friday and Christmas) from 9:00 a.m. to 4:45 p.m. Backstage tours, lasting 90 minutes, are offered Sundays only. They start from the Music Room-Exhibition foyer on the ground level; tickets are A$10.

A better way to appreciate the Opera House is to take in a performance. You can get a full schedule of all events at most visitor centers. The Opera House box office is open Monday through Saturday from 9:00 a.m. to 8:30 p.m. and Sunday from 9:00 a.m. to 4:00 p.m. You can also book by phone (with a major credit card) by calling 250-7178 or 250-7163.

▲▲**Sydney Tower** rises 1,000 feet above the Centrepoint shopping complex off Market Street between Pitt and Castlereagh streets. Some Aussie cynics call this edifice "the bucket on the stick," but as the highest public building in the Southern Hemisphere, it's worth the trip up for the view. Open 9:30 a.m. to 9:30 p.m. Monday through Saturday, 10:30 a.m. to 6:30 p.m. Sundays and holidays, closed Christmas. It will cost you A$6 to take the lift up. Lunch and dinner are served in a pair of restaurants immediately below the observation deck.

▲▲**Hyde Park Barracks** is on Queen's Square at the top of Macquarie Street. Designed by convict architect Francis Greenway (whose picture is on the A$10 bill) and erected in 1819 as a dormitory for male convicts, it has become an interesting museum of Sydney social history. Start on the top floor to learn in considerable detail about the shipment of convicts from England to Sydney, then step down to the second floor to trace the city's nineteenth-century development. Open 10:00 a.m. to 5:00 p.m. daily (12:00 noon to 5:00 p.m. Tuesday); closed Good Friday and Christmas. Free admission.

▲**The Old Mint** is next door to the Barracks. One of Australia's oldest public buildings (1817), it was built as a hospital wing but became the first branch of the British Royal Mint outside of London after gold was discovered in 1851. Since 1982, it has been an elegant, well-organized museum of decorative art, coins, and stamps. Open 10:00 a.m. to 5:00 p.m. daily (12:00 noon to 5:00 p.m. Wednesday); closed Good Friday and Christmas. Free admission.

▲**Art Gallery of New South Wales**, Art Gallery Road, The Domain, is Sydney's (but not Australia's) best art museum. It is interesting for its survey of Aussie paintings through the nineteenth and twentieth centuries. A major expansion a few years ago added a sculpture terrace, an Asian art gallery, and several theaters. Open 10:00 a.m. to 5:00 p.m. daily (12:00 noon to 5:00 p.m. Sunday); closed Good Friday and Christmas. Free admission.

▲**Royal Botanic Gardens**, the second botanic gardens in the Southern Hemisphere, is a pleasant place for a stroll or a picnic. Open 8:00 a.m. to sunset daily. Free guided walks are conducted at 9:30 a.m. Wednesday and 10:00 a.m. Friday from the visitor center. Free admission.

▲▲**The Australian Museum**, located at the corner of

William and College streets opposite Hyde Park, is of special interest for superb exhibits of Aboriginal and Papua New Guinean life-styles. It also has good displays of Australian geological and natural history, as well as a Pacific art gallery. Open 10:00 a.m. to 5:00 p.m. daily (12:00 noon to 5:00 p.m. Monday); closed Good Friday and Christmas. Admission A$4; $2 Sundays; free after 4 p.m.

▲▲**Darling Harbour**, a 133-acre urban redevelopment project on the west end of downtown Sydney, opened in 1988 to acclaim. Connected by monorail to the city center, it is built around a central park and Chinese garden and includes a convention and exhibition center, a hotel/casino, 30 restaurants, 200 retail shops, and an entertainment center. Also within the complex are the **Australian National Maritime Museum**, open 9:00 a.m. to 5:00 p.m. daily (admission A$7), and **Sydney Aquarium**, which claims to be the world's largest (open 9:30 a.m. to 9:00 p.m. daily; admission A$12.50).

▲▲**The Powerhouse**, adjacent to Darling Harbour at Harris and Mary Ann streets in Ultimo, is an impressive science and technology museum that opened for the Bicentennial in 1988. Displays—many of them "hands-on"—cover everything from steam engines to the space race to the history of the brewing industry in New South Wales. Open 10:00 a.m. to 5:00 p.m. daily except Christmas. Admission A$5.

▲**Elizabeth Bay House**, Onslow Avenue, Elizabeth Bay. Close to Kings Cross but on the Sydney Explorer bus route, this elegant 1835 colonial mansion has been fully restored to period decor. Open 10:00 a.m. to 4:30 p.m. Tuesday through Sunday. Adult admission A$4.

▲▲▲**The Rocks**, Sydney's most historic district, is located just northwest of Circular Quay. The oldest building still standing, Cadmans Cottage, was built in 1816, but most structures date from the 1840s to 1880s, during which time this was Sydney's main commercial and maritime quarter.

To see the area properly, you should guide yourself on

a walking tour beginning from The Rocks Visitor Centre, 104 George Street (see "Helpful Hints," Day 1). You can pick up a map describing various sites, but the best way to explore is simply to amble and browse, ducking into the various small shops, art galleries, museums, and pubs. Don't miss the new **Museum of Contemporary Art**, on George Street near Circular Quay, a handsome Art Deco building with a fascinating modern collection (open 11:00 a.m. to 7:00 p.m. daily except Tuesday; admission A$6). Several pubs, including The Old Push, Phillips Foote, the Lord Nelson, and the venerable Hero of Waterloo feature live "trad jazz" performances during after-work "happy hour" and on weekends.

The highlight of The Rocks is the **Argyle Centre**, a four-story complex of various artisans' galleries, antique shops, and cafés. (It was undergoing a major renovation in 1993.) Housed in a group of 1828 sandstone bond stores and warehouses, it authentically preserves the atmosphere of the period—and nowhere better than the **Argyle Tavern**, a great spot for an Australian night out. As you fill up on Sydney rock oysters, grilled barramundi, or steak-and-kidney pie, the Jolly Swagman show will introduce you to a variety of Aussie bush ballads and folk songs, the Aboriginal *dijeridu* (a primitive droning instrument), and the fine art of shearing a sheep—right on stage. Showtime is 8:00 to 9:30 nightly; come by 7:30 to place your order and beat the rush. A warning: shoestring travelers may want to think twice before purging their wallets of A$50 (per person) for the dinner and show.

MORE OF SYDNEY

I'd spend today touring the eastern suburbs, but there are many other options. Take the ferry to Manly and the zoo, for instance, or travel to the Blue Mountains or the Hunter Valley.

Suggested Schedule

9:00 a.m.	Take the subway (Blue Line) to Bondi Junction, then catch bus No. 380 or 389 to Bondi Beach. You'll arrive by 9:30 a.m., giving you two hours to soak in rays and surf culture before lunch.
11:30 a.m.	Catch a city bus north up the coast to Watson's Bay for a seafood lunch at Doyle's.
1:30 p.m.	Bus No. 325 heads back toward the city. Stop off at Vaucluse House, an 1830s mansion.
2:30 p.m.	Disembark in Double Bay for a look at Sydney's version of Rodeo Drive.
3:30 p.m.	Have a cab drop you in Paddington at the New Edition Bookshop, 328 Oxford Street, where you can obtain free "The Paddington Book" with a map and suggested walking tour.
5:30 p.m.	Continue to the Cross by foot, bus, or taxi. It's your night to paint the town red.

Sightseeing Highlights
▲▲**Bondi** (pronounced Bond-eye) is the most famous of all Sydney's beaches. It's not the most attractive, unless perhaps you're talking about the topless south end of the beach, but there seems to be more tradition and a livelier crowd here than at other eastern suburbs beaches, especially during summer when surf lifesaving contests are held throughout Australia.

▲**Vaucluse House**, Olala Avenue, Vaucluse, was built in 1803 and became the home of William Charles Wentworth, the Thomas Jefferson of Australia, from 1827 to 1853. A beachfront manor that sits in 27 acres of park and garden, it has been lavishly refurbished in the style of Wentworth's time. Open 10:00 a.m. to 4:30 p.m. Tuesday through Sunday. Admission A$4.

▲**Double Bay** may be Australia's most fashionable few blocks. Knox Street, Cross Street, and New South Head Road are lined with designer boutiques, exclusive jewelers, and antique shops. You'll see Sydney's beautiful people sizing each other up at sidewalk cafés and delis.

▲▲**Paddington** may be downmarket from Double Bay, but it's upmarket from most of the rest of Sydney. Known locally as "Paddo," this hilly neighborhood might strike Washingtonians as being a little like Georgetown. Here, the young, upwardly mobile population has put its restoration energies into Victorian terrace houses rather than brownstone manors. Many artists, musicians, and educators live among the trendy arts and crafts galleries and numerous fine restaurants and pubs.

Special attractions in Paddington include an open-air market called the **Village Bazaar**, held from 10:00 a.m. to 4:00 p.m. every Saturday at the corner of Newcombe and Oxford streets, and the **Victoria Barracks**, a superb example of British colonial military architecture on Oxford Street opposite Hopewell Street. If you're here on Tuesday, see the impressive changing of the guard at 11:00 a.m.

▲**Manly** is a good destination for those who prefer to spend time on the water instead of in trains and buses. Spread across a narrow neck of land separating the harbor from the Tasman Sea, it has a quaint pedestrian mall connecting the famed surfing beach with a still-water swimming area. Manly's attractions include **Marineland** (open 10:00 a.m. to 5:00 p.m. daily), an amusement pier, a series of waterslides, and an art gallery/museum. Manly is easily reached from Circular Quay by ferry (A$6 round trip) or hydrofoil (A$9 round trip).

▲**Taronga Park Zoo**, Bradleys Head Road, Mosman, is an excellent place to get an introduction to Australia's unique wildlife. Its exhibits include a treetop koala exhibit, a platypus house, a rain forest aviary, and a special nocturnal house. You can travel there either by ferry from Circular Quay (A$2.50 each way) or by Bus No. 237 or 238 across the Sydney Harbour Bridge. Open daily year-round, 9:00 a.m. to 5:00 p.m. Admission is A$12.70, or just 50 cents more when purchased as part of a round-trip ferry ticket.

Birkenhead Point, a shopping center off Victoria Road in the harborside suburb of Drummoyne, a few miles west of the city center, might be considered a rainy day alternative. There are some 130 shops and restaurants, plus the **Lego Centre**, one of only two permanent exhibitions in the world of models built from these children's building blocks. Open daily 9:15 a.m. to 5:15 p.m., Thursdays until 9:00 p.m.

Day Trips from Sydney

If you're inclined to rent your car a day early, here are some worthwhile day trip options.

▲**The Blue Mountains**, once a foreboding natural barrier to early settlers, are now a favorite weekend getaway for Sydneysiders. Their undeclared capital is Katoomba, a small town 106 km (66 miles) west of Sydney, though they spread from Penrith to Lithgow. The mountains' most famous attraction is the **Three Sisters**, an unusual rock formation associated with Aboriginal legend. A cable car and scenic railway at the site make it a honeymooners' delight. There are also spectacular caves and waterfalls, art galleries, and historic museums.

▲**Pittwater** and **Broken Bay**, at the mouth of the Hawkesbury River marking the northern boundary of the Sydney metropolis, are places of great natural beauty. They're best seen from the deck of a private yacht, but they can also be thoroughly appreciated from the land. Drive north up Sydney's east coast through Mona Vale to **Palm Beach**, or better yet, spend an afternoon bushwalking in **Ku-ring-gai Chase National Park**.

▲**Old Sydney Town**, near Gosford about 70 km (43 miles) north of downtown Sydney, re-creates the Sydney Cove settlement as it is thought to have been in the early 1800s. Only authentic materials and methods were used in building the 50-acre theme park. Soldiers, convicts, and free settlers, all in period costume, continually act out scenes from the colony's history. Open 10:00 a.m. to 5:00 p.m. Wednesday through Sunday; daily during school holidays. Admission is A$12.80. A rail tour, leaving Sydney's Central Station at 8:09 a.m. and returning shortly after 6:05 p.m., costs A$30 for adults and includes admission.

▲**The Hunter Valley**, near Cessnock some 180 km (100 miles) north of Sydney, is Australia's oldest wine-producing district and its second most important (after the Barossa Valley near Adelaide). The 34 wineries here are best known for their soft reds. Most are open for tastings daily from 9:00 or 10:00 a.m. to about 5:00 p.m. Hungerford Hill, Rothbury Estate, Tyrrells, and Wyndham Estate are among the most highly regarded.

Nightlife

Anything and everything goes in **Kings Cross**, several meandering blocks of burlesque shows, theater restaurants, discotheques, tattoo parlors, and streetwalkers where Darlinghurst Road, Victoria Street, Bayswater Road, and William Street come together a mile east of the city center. Some call the Cross "bohemian," others "sleazy"; the truth may lie somewhere between. People-watching is the best form of entertainment here; grab a window table and a cup of cappuccino at an open-air café.

To find out what's happening on any given day in the greater Sydney area, get hold of the *Sydney Morning Herald*'s Friday "Metro" section, with listings of the entertainment week ahead. Musical offerings are broken down into classical, jazz, country, folk, acoustic, and rock, with the latter category as large as the other five combined.

There are especially large concentrations of music pubs in Paddington (try the **Grand National Hotel** or the **Windsor Castle Hotel**) and Bondi (the **Royal Hotel** is best), but you'll find them everywhere.

The best modern jazz in Sydney may be found at **'Round Midnight**, 2 Roslyn Street, Kings Cross. For good rock in a trendy atmosphere, check out the **Oz Rock Café**, 248 William Street, Kings Cross, or the ubiquitous **Hard Rock Café**, 121 Crown Street, Darlinghurst.

If you're strictly into meeting people without having to shout over the din of music, check out some of the city's wine bars—like **French's** on Oxford Street in Darlinghurst, **Soren's** in Woolloomooloo, or **The Stoned Crow** in Crow's Nest, across the Harbour Bridge. In North Sydney you'll also find **Sheila's**, a singles bar with provocative coasters that read, "If you're looking for a friend, leave this side up."

Live theater is extremely popular in Sydney. Aside from the Opera House, you can take in fine productions at the **Theatre Royal** on Castlereagh Street, the **Wharf Theatre** on Pier 4 (near The Rocks), and others. Lower George Street has the greatest concentration of cinema houses for moviegoers. All major studio American films are shown here, but don't miss an opportunity to see some of the outstanding movies made in Australia today.

An Australian phenomenon is the Leagues Club, of which rugby league clubs and returned servicemen's league clubs are most prevalent. Depending upon their size, they usually include a small gambling casino (with slot machines), a restaurant and bar, and an entertainment lounge, often with live music on weekends. This is where the working man typically takes his wife or girlfriend for a night out. While they are membership clubs, overseas visitors are normally welcome. Two of the biggest are the **South Sydney Junior Rugby League Club**, 556 Anzac Parade, Kingsford, and the **St. George Leagues Club**, 124 Princes Highway, Kogarah.

SYDNEY TO CANBERRA

Leave Australia's queen city and drive south to Canberra, the national capital, pausing en route at historic Gledswood Homestead and Berrima. In Canberra, take time for an overview of the foundation and continuing evolution of this attractive, specially created city.

Suggested Schedule	
8:00 a.m.	Pick up your reserved rental car and head out of Sydney via the Hume Highway.
9:30 a.m.	Arrive at Gledswood Homestead and wander through the working colonial farm.
10:45 a.m.	Leave for Berrima.
11:30 a.m.	Explore Berrima, a sandstone-and-brick village appearing very much today as it did in 1831. Lunch at the Surveyor General Inn, the oldest continuously licensed pub in Australia.
1:30 p.m.	Leave for Canberra.
3:30 p.m.	On arrival, drive straight to the Canberra Planning Exhibition on Lake Burley Griffin. Study the models and see the video to understand the grand plan for this twentieth-century capital.
4:30 p.m.	Capture the view from the top of Mount Ainslie.
5:00 p.m.	Move into your accommodation. Spend a quiet evening or take in the theater or a nightclub.

Leaving Sydney
When you obtain your rental car, double-check to be certain your agent has provided you with a Gregory's or UBD street guide to Sydney. That's your passport out of the metropolis in case you get lost.

Most visitors get their car at a rental agent on William Street, between Kings Cross and downtown. Proceed

west through Hyde Park, turn left on Pitt Street, and follow the signs to Liverpool. The Hume Highway, Route
31, branches south (to the left) off the Great Western
Highway near Summer Hill, 8 km from William Street.

The Hume Highway
Soon after leaving Liverpool, about 30 km from the
Hume Highway junction, the highway becomes a four-
lane freeway. It stays that way (with only a couple of
slowdowns) all the way to Canberra—in fact, to
Melbourne—enabling you to drive the 294 km (183
miles) from Sydney to the capital in 3 hours, if you so
choose.

Our tour route, however, involves a few diversions. At
the point where the freeway begins, turn right on Route
89, Camden Valley Way (the Old Hume Highway), to the
community of Catherine Field. It's about 10 km farther to
the historic **Gledswood Homestead** built in 1810 by
convict labor and now classified by the National Trust
and the Heritage Commission. Guided tours of the homestead, winery (in a former coach house), and working
farm are offered daily from 10:00 a.m. to 5:00 p.m. Sheep
shearing, boomerang throwing, and other demonstrations
are often presented. Admission A$5.

▲▲**Berrima** is bypassed by the new freeway, making its
colonial isolation all the more appealing. Situated 128 km
(80 miles) from Sydney and 166 km (103 miles) from
Canberra, this village (founded in 1831) is a historical
gem. Pick up a walking tour map at the Georgian-style
courthouse, where the first jury trial in the New South
Wales colony was held in 1843. (It's open 10:00 a.m. to
4:00 p.m. daily; admission is A60 cents.) The **jail**, built in
1839, closed in 1902 but reopened in 1949 after extensive
reconstruction (and still in use), was one of the most
feared in Australia in the mid-nineteenth century.

About two dozen government buildings, early church-
es, and private manors have survived the passage of
time. Many of them contain galleries, antique and crafts

shops, and restaurants and cafés serving Devonshire teas. At the **Surveyor General Inn**, which celebrated its 158th anniversary in business in 1992, you can cook your own steak lunch, pile it high with offerings from a salad bar and potatoes, and wash it down with a beer for under A$10.

A further diversion off the Hume Highway from Berrima would lead you through the charming village of **Bundanoon** on the edge of lush Morton National Park. Time's a-wastin', however. Return to the freeway, drive right on through the big farming center of Goulburn (pop. 25,000), waving at the campy "world's largest Merino sheep" sculpture as you pass. Twelve km farther on, bear left onto the Federal Highway and slide by the rim of large (but usually dry) Lake George into the Australian Capital Territory.

Canberra Orientation

Visitors often find Canberra like a tree without roots, a building without a foundation. Indeed, the city is too young to have developed much heritage of its own. Like Washington, D.C., Canberra, A.C.T., is very much a government town—but its 280,000 people haven't had a 187-year history to develop a feeling of heritage. It wasn't until 1901 that Melbourne and Sydney, throwing up their political arms in frustration over persistent squabbling for the right to be the national capital, finally compromised and agreed to construct a new city between the two metropolises.

In 1912, an American architect named Walter Burley Griffin won an international contest to design the capital. Following his plans, 2,366 square km (912 square miles) of sheep-grazing land were transformed into the Australian Capital Territory, and within that plot, the new city of Canberra was built. (The name "Canberra" was derived from an Aboriginal term meaning "meeting place.") In 1927, all government functions were moved here from Melbourne.

Burley Griffin's grandiose plan has taken far longer
to complete than anyone imagined. Between two world
wars, a Great Depression, and much political infighting,
construction funds have been hard to come by. In fact,
Canberra is only now being completed to the architect's
specifications! After 60 years of legislative debates in a
provisional parliament house, a magnificent new
Parliament House was finished just in time for the
Australian Bicentennial in 1988.

Canberra's design carefully balances natural features—low, bush-cloaked mountains and lovely, meandering Lake Burley Griffin—with geometrical patterns,
mainly a series of concentric circles interconnected by
strong lines. Capital Hill, site of the new Parliament, and
City Hill, around which most commercial functions
revolve, are 3 km apart, linked across the deep blue
lake by Commonwealth Avenue. Each "hill" is the hub
of a series of streets that spread from the center like the
spokes of a wheel.

Northbourne Avenue, on which you'll arrive from the
north, runs straight as an arrow for over 4 km directly
to City Hill. Soon after you circumnavigate the hill but
before crossing the lake, look for directional signs to
the **Canberra Planning Exhibition** on Regatta Point,
operated by the National Capital Planning Authority. Put
preconceived notions aside; if you have any interest in
the creative process, it isn't boring. In effect, it's a historical museum, describing with text, photographs, and
audiovisual presentation the creation of Canberra from
virtually uninhabited bush. A huge, three-dimensional
model of the city helps you locate points of interest.
Open 9:00 a.m. to 5:00 p.m. daily except Christmas;
admission is free. A snack bar and souvenir shop are on
a terrace overlooking the lake.

Of several hills with lookouts over the city, the
best—from the standpoint of understanding Canberra's
layout—is **Mount Ainslie** in the northeast quadrant.
Not only is it the highest at 842 meters (2,772 feet);

from the top, you can look straight down across the stalwart Australian War Memorial to Anzac Parade, which neatly bisects the Federal Triangle and affords a direct view of the provisional and new Parliament Houses.

The highest viewpoint in Canberra is actually atop the striking 195-meter (640-foot) Telecom Tower on **Black Mountain** west of City Hill. But unless you dine in the revolving restaurant, you'll have to pay A$2 to gain access to the three public viewing galleries. Another lookout is on **Red Hill**, south of Capital Hill, with a restaurant offering panoramic views of the southern suburbs.

Canberra's climate, quite logically, is unlike that of any of the seaside state capitals. Located about 160 km (95 miles) inland and at 580 meters (1,900 feet) elevation in a spur of the Great Dividing Range, its summers are hotter and drier than other major cities and its winters colder, with occasional (if rare) snow flurries.

City Transportation
If you arrive in Canberra without a car at the airport, railway depot, or bus station, you're not stranded. The ACTION public bus network runs through the city and its suburbs from 6:00 a.m. to 11:30 p.m. daily (8:30 a.m. to 6:30 p.m. Sunday), with fares of A$1.40 to most destinations. No. 905 operates to Regatta Point; No. 302 runs from the city to the Australian War Memorial; No. 357 connects City Hill with the rail station via the National Library and provisional Parliament House; No. 380 plies the 8 km (5 miles) between the youth hostel and downtown.

Better designed for the tourist is the **Canberra Explorer**. This unmistakable bright red bus runs its narrated 25-km (15½-mile) circuit seven times every day from 10:15 a.m. to 4:15 p.m., making scheduled stops at major attractions and hotels. You can buy a day ticket for A$9, allowing you to disembark anywhere and reboard an hour or two later, or pay A$4.50 for a one-hour tour.

Where to Stay
The greatest concentration of accommodations in all price categories is along Northbourne Avenue, the main thoroughfare entering Canberra from the north.

Regarded by some as the best is **The Pavilion**, on National Circuit at Canberra Avenue, Forrest, ACT 2603 (tel. 295-3144). Somewhat less expensive, with a garden atmosphere, is the **Canberra International**, 242 Northbourne Avenue, Dickson, ACT 2602 (tel. 247-6966). I'm happy in the moderate price range at **Down Town Spero's Motel**, 82 Northbourne Avenue, Canberra, ACT 2601 (tel. 249-1388), an easy three-block stroll from the commercial center around City Hill.

You'll find adequate economy-class lodging at **Tall Trees Lodge**, 21 Stephen Street, Ainslie, ACT 2602 (tel. 247-9200). The **Gowrie Private Hotel**, 210 Northbourne Avenue, Braddon, ACT 2602 (tel. 249-6033), has twin 10-story towers containing 569 simple rooms and a big, round-floor cafeteria. True budget accommodations are hard to come by in Canberra, but the **National Memorial Youth Hostel** is on Dryandra Street in O'Connor, ACT 2601 (tel. 248-9759).

Where to Eat
The most central area for dining is Garema Place, a spacious pedestrian mall east of Northbourne Avenue and north of London Circuit, just above City Hill. There's a wide range of choices here, from candlelit meals to fast-food takeaway. **Dorette's Bistro**, upstairs at 17 Garema Place (near Bunda Street), is a self-styled Bohemian café with live classical and jazz music on alternate nights. **Mama's Trattoria**, 7 Garema Place, offers big pasta meals for no more than A$7. A couple of blocks away is the 24-hour **Lovely Lady Pancake Parlour**, East Row and Alinga Street, with full meals at A$6 to A$8 and a bottomless coffee cup. Not far away, near City Hill on Northbourne Avenue, the **Private Bin** at No. 50 offers bistro menus and entertainment. Vegetarians congregate at the **Honeydew**, 55 Northbourne Avenue.

In the Kingston district near Capital Hill, **Innovations**, 35 Kennedy Street, serves native Australian cuisine (like kangaroo and witchety grubs!) for a high price tag. **Café Leila**, on Jardine Street, has pasta and salads for much lower cost.

Worthy of special note are **Tilley Devine's Café Gallery**, 96 Wattle Street, Lynehan, a feminist-operated establishment that doesn't admit men unless accompanied by women; the **Canberra Tradesmen's Union Club**, Badham Street, Dickson, with reasonably priced bistro meals served in restored trams; and a pair of cafeterias in Australian National University's student center, the **ANU Refectory** and the **Asian Bistro**.

Helpful Hints

The **A.C.T. Tourism Commission** (tel. 245-6464) has its main offices in the Jolimont Centre at 65-67 Northbourne Avenue near London Circuit. It's open weekdays 8:30 a.m. to 5:15 p.m., Saturday 9:00 a.m. to 5:00 p.m., and Sunday 9:00 a.m. to 1:30 p.m. More convenient for those driving into town from the north is the **Visitor Information Centre**, on Northbourne Avenue just south of the junction of the Federal and Barton highways, open daily (except Christmas) from 9:00 a.m. to 5:00 p.m.

The **Central Post Office** adjoins the Jolimont Centre at Alinga and Moore streets. **Banks** are open from 9:30 a.m. to 4:00 p.m. Monday through Thursday, an hour later on Friday. Shops are generally open 9:00 a.m. to 5:30 p.m. Monday through Friday, 9:00 a.m. to 4:00 p.m. Saturday. (Some stay open later Friday nights but close by noon Saturdays.)

The elegant **U.S. Embassy** is at 21 Moonah Place in Yarralumla, near Capital Hill (tel. 270-5000). The **Canadian High Commission** is on Commonwealth Avenue (tel. 273-3844).

In case of emergencies, dial 000.

CANBERRA

Explore the national capital. Start at the new Parliament House; if the Senate and House of Representatives are in session, you can view the proceedings from a public gallery. Take a drive through the Yarralumla area to see the impressive row of national embassies, then lunch at the High Court, inspect the National Gallery, and visit the Australian War Memorial Museum.

Suggested Schedule	
9:30 a.m.	Get in line for a 10:00 a.m. session of the Senate or House of Representatives at the new Parliament House.
11:00 a.m.	Drive through Canberra's "Embassy Row."
12:00 noon	Visit the High Court and have lunch in the café.
1:30 p.m.	Peruse the Australian National Gallery.
3:00 p.m.	Spend a couple of hours at the Australian War Memorial Museum.
5:00 p.m.	Hire a canoe for a trip on Lake Burley Griffin or return to your hotel and relax.
7:00 p.m.	Dine in Garema Place.

Sightseeing Highlights
▲▲▲**The New Parliament House**, with its memorable A\$4 million flagpole, was officially opened on May 9, 1988, by Queen Elizabeth II. The designers—the American firm of Mitchell/Giurgola and Australian architect Richard Thorp—kept intact Walter Burley Griffin's original plan for Canberra with gently curving walls and careful landscaping, picking up the axis pattern of earlier roads and buildings. The 266-foot, four-legged flagpole is intended to be the emblem of Australian government.

The building's architecture follows the circular contours of Capital Hill with curved walls and a grassy walkway over the top of the gently sloping roof. The House of

Representatives lies on the east side of the walls, the
Senate on the west. The main public entry is from the
north, past a ceremonial pool. Works of Australian art are
incorporated in the interior design, including an
Aboriginal mosaic in the Forecourt. All told, the massive
structure covers 79 acres and contains 450 separate rooms.
It cost just over A$1,000 million to build.

Parliament is in session from March to November.
Business is conducted in the traditional "Westminster"
fashion. Sessions commence at 2:00 p.m. Monday and
Tuesday, 10:00 a.m. and 2:00 p.m. Wednesday, 10:00 a.m.
and 8:00 p.m. Thursday, and 9:00 a.m. (Senate) or 10:00
a.m. (House) and again at 2:00 p.m. on Friday. There's no
admission, but you may need advance bookings to sit in
the House's popular gallery. (Call 277-4889 on arrival in
Canberra.) Arrive a little early to get in line. You'll be
admitted on a first-come, first-served basis; your visit will
be limited to 25 minutes if there's a crowd waiting. On
days when Parliament does not sit, there are free tours of
the complex every half-hour from 9 a.m. to 5 p.m.

▲**The Provisional Parliament House**, never intended to
be more than a temporary capitol, was the seat of
Australia's federal government from 1927 to 1988. A grace-
ful white building in a parklike setting on King George
Terrace, it is now being converted to a constitutional
museum. Inside is a gallery of oil portraits of Queen
Elizabeth II, past governors-general, and parliamentarians.

▲**Embassy Row** really doesn't exist as such, but the
Yarralumla section of Canberra, just west of Capital Hill,
has the highest concentration of foreign embassies in
Australia. Most are elegant edifices reflecting national
architectural tastes and easily viewed from the winding
residential roads. Few are open to visitors except on offi-
cial business, but the **Indonesian Embassy**, 80 Darwin
Avenue, has a pavilion displaying crafts and musical
instruments open daily from 10:00 a.m. to 12:30 p.m. and
2:00 to 4:00 p.m., and the **High Commission of Papua
New Guinea**, Forster Crescent, has a display of trade and
cultural items open weekdays from 9:00 a.m. to 12:30 p.m.

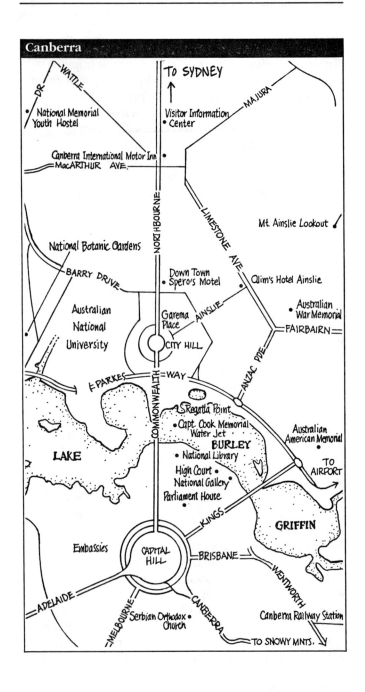

and 2:30 to 4:30 p.m.

▲▲**The High Court of Australia**, in an impressive con-
crete-and-glass structure on the shore of Lake Burley
Griffin, is the nation's ultimate court of appeal. The Great
Hall—the main public area—has two huge murals depicting the justice system and the states. Ramps connect it with
courtrooms on three succeeding floors, decorated with
indigenous woodwork, woven tapestries, sculptures, and
other native artworks. When in session, the court sits from
10:15 a.m. to 12:45 p.m. and 2:15 to 4:15 p.m. weekdays.
The building is open free to visitors 9:45 a.m. to 4:30 p.m.
most days. A licensed café, overlooking Lake Burley
Griffin, serves excellent light meals for less than A$10.

▲▲**The Australian National Gallery**, connected by a
first-floor walkway to the High Court building, has a fine
collection of Australian and foreign paintings, sculpture,
and decorative arts. Free guided tours of the Australian art
section are offered daily at 11:15 a.m. and 2:15 p.m. The
gallery is open 10:00 a.m. to 5:00 p.m. daily except Good
Friday and Christmas; admission is A$3.

▲**The National Library of Australia**, west of the High
Court on the lakefront, has an Australian art collection of its
own, displayed daily from 9:00 a.m. to 4:45 p.m. in the Rex
Nan Kivell Room. Some 3.6 million books are stored in 10
acres of space and on 47 miles of shelves. The main reading room is open to the public 9:30 a.m. to 10:00 p.m.
Monday through Thursday, 9:30 a.m. to 4:45 p.m. Friday
and Saturday, and 1:30 to 4:45 p.m. Sunday.

**Questacon—The National Science & Technology
Centre**, next door to the National Library, is a hands-on
museum comprising six exhibition galleries, two theaters, a
science shop, and more than 150 experiments and displays.
Open daily 10:00 a.m. to 5:00 p.m. Admission A$6.

▲▲▲**The Australian War Memorial** is the country's best
museum of any kind. Whether you view war as glorious,
horrible, or a bit of both, this somber memorial will make a
definite impression. Inscribed with the names of more than
102,000 Australians who died in service to their country, it
stares straight down tree-lined Anzac Parade and across

Lake Burley Griffin at Parliament House, 4 km (2 miles)
distant. Built in the 1930s and expanded often since, the
museum/art gallery traces Aussie military history from
British colonial times through the World War I tragedy of
Gallipoli and the World War II attacks on Darwin to
Australia's more modern involvement in the Vietnam con-
flict. Guided tours are available weekdays at 10:30 a.m.
and 1:30 p.m. Open daily 9:00 a.m. to 4:45 p.m. Free
admission.

▲**Lake Burley Griffin**, the vivid blue centerpiece of
Canberra, is highlighted by the Captain Cook Memorial
Water Jet (sending a column of water 430 feet above the
lake from 10:00 a.m. to 12:00 noon and again 2:00 to 4:00
p.m. daily) and the Carillon (a 53-bell tower with free
recitals on Wednesdays, Sundays, and holidays). You can
cruise the lake for an hour or two aboard the *City of
Canberra* or *Lady Claire* (leaving at 11:45 a.m. and 1:00
p.m. daily, cost A$8 to A$12), or rent a rowboat, canoe,
paddle boat, or sailboard (A$10 to A$14 an hour). All
water activities are centered on West Basin in Acton Park.

Nightlife
Canberra's evening activity has improved in recent years,
with outdoor cafés open late and a sizable range of theaters and nightclubs. **Rascals**, in Petrie Plaza, City, is the
top nightclub. Things liven up a bit on Friday and
Saturday night, when several small bars and taverns feature live entertainment for dancing. Most residents find
their diversions at RSL, leagues or other clubs in Canberra
or neighboring Queanbeyan, N.S.W. Visitors are welcome
to check out the **Canberra Labor Club**, Chandler Street
in Belconnen; the **Canberra Workers Club**, University
Avenue and Children's Street, City; or the **Royals Rugby
Union Football Club**, Weston Creek.

The modern **Canberra Theatre Centre** in Civic
Square, off London Circuit, contains a theater, playhouse,
gallery, restaurant, and rehearsal room. Everything from
serious drama to a world-class ballet to Gilbert and
Sullivan to rock concerts is presented here.

CANBERRA TO BEECHWORTH

Today's route leads past the alpine resort of Thredbo in the Snowy Mountains via Corryong—reputed home of poet Banjo Paterson's "Man from Snowy River"—to Beechworth, a town straight out of the nineteenth-century gold rush.

Suggested Schedule	
8:30 a.m.	Leave Canberra, driving via Cooma to Thredbo.
11:30 a.m.	Arrive at Thredbo. Take an hour for lunch and a look around, or buy some sandwich makings and stop for a picnic farther down the road.
2:30 p.m.	After a drive down the Alpine Way through the Snowy Mountains, visit tiny Corryong.
4:30 p.m.	Arrive in Yackandandah for a short tour of this village classified by the National Trust.
5:30 p.m.	Reach Beechworth, whose main street has changed little in 100 years.

Today's Drive
Follow the signs off Canberra Avenue, southeast of Capital Hill, to reach Route 23, the Monaro Highway. **Cooma**, 117 km (73 miles) south of Canberra, is about a 1-hour drive. Often considered the "gateway" to the Snowy Mountains because most skiers pass through it en route to the various resorts, this town of 8,000 also is headquarters of the Snowy Mountains Hydro-Electric Scheme, a massive project that created dams, power stations, and high-altitude lakes throughout the range west of here.
▲**Thredbo**, another 96 km (53 miles) of winding road west across the Snowy River, is built like a Tyrolean village with chalets dotting its alpine slopes. Regarded as Australia's No. 1 ski resort, it is also a popular summer escape with the country's highest golf course (1,370

meters, or 4,495 feet), tennis courts, and horse-riding trails. Looming above the snowfields at the top of its Crackenback chair lift is Australia's highest peak, Mount Kosciusko, 2,229 meters (7,313 feet) in elevation. It's an easy walk for summer day-hikers and winter "lang-laufers" (cross-country skiers). Nonskiers find spring the best time to visit, when the slopes are covered with wildflowers. Twenty separate lodges and a youth hostel provide beds and/or meals for skiers and other vacationers. The Thredbo Alpine Hotel, at the foot of the mountain, is a good choice for lunch with a view.

▲▲**Alpine Way** runs for 74 km (46 mi.) through Kosciusko National Park from Thredbo to Khancoban. There is a A\$5 admission fee to the park. More than half of the route is gravel, but it's well graded and is not normally (snow or heavy rain excepted) a difficult or dangerous drive. It's tremendously scenic, offering numerous vistas of the dense bush surrounding the headwaters of the Murray River, Australia's longest. On the off chance you've thrown a fishing pole in with your gear, the streams and lakes along this road are a good place to cast a line. Buy a license as you pass through Cooma (A\$10 for 30 days).

An alternative route in winter, or at any other time that Alpine Way is impassable, is to travel northwest from Cooma on the Snowy Mountains Highway, along the shores of manmade Lake Eucumbene, through the village of Adaminaby (with its preposterous mammoth sculpture of a rainbow trout), to Kiandra, where gold miners raced on skis as early as 1859. Turn south here through Cabramurra and several Snowy River Scheme lookouts to rejoin Alpine Way at Khancoban.

Upon reaching **Khancoban**, a tiny township established for hydroelectric workers, you will have dropped nearly 3,500 feet from Thredbo. Follow the signs across the Murray River into the state of Victoria. It's 21 km (13 miles) to **Corryong**.

A broad main street establishes the character of this country center. Be sure to read Paterson's "The Man from Snowy River" before you arrive. Jack Riley, generally

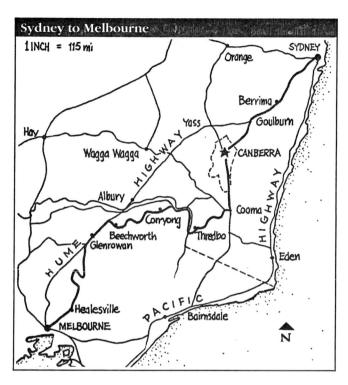

regarded as the model for the poem (and the movie), made his home in Corryong and is buried in the town cemetery. He and his legend are remembered at the **Man from Snowy River Folk Museum** with an eclectic but charming variety of exhibits. Located at the west end of town, it's open only from 2:00 to 4:00 p.m. Monday through Saturday. Admission is A$2.

Rather than backtracking on the Murray Valley Highway, proceed directly west about 120 km (75 miles) via Tallangatta to **Yackandandah**. (You can avoid the bottleneck of the Albury-Wodonga area by cutting over to the Kiewa Valley Highway near Tangambalanga.) So important is Yackandandah, historically and architecturally, that the entire township and surrounding hills are classified by the National Trust. Why the hills? Because the creeks and old gold diggings still yield alluvial gold to amateur prospectors. Take a few minutes to stroll the tree-lined avenues of town and photograph the buildings.

Beechworth

The most historically interesting town in northeast Victoria is Beechworth, 24 km (15 miles) southwest of Yackandandah. Established in 1839, it soon became one of Australia's richest goldfields, yielding 4.1 million ounces between 1852 and 1862. Commercial mining continued until 1920, and weekend panners still find gold in the creeks today.

By the time you arrive, the visitor information center in The Rock Cavern, at Ford and Camp streets, will probably be closed. You can take a "formal" self-guided tour tomorrow morning. For now, check into an accommodation with appropriate frontier atmosphere, dine, and get some shut-eye.

Where to Stay

Rose Cottage Bed and Breakfast, 42 Camp Street (tel. 057/28-1069), is a quaint four-bedroom home fully furnished with Victorian antiques. The price of A$46 single, A$70 double, includes a full breakfast. Next door, the more commonplace but comfortable **Carriage Motor Inn**, 44 Camp Street (tel. 28-1830), with similar prices.

Tanswell's Commercial Hotel, 30 Ford Street (tel. 28-1480), 122 years old, has rooms with toilets down the hall for A$25 single, A$35 double, including breakfast. (Superb dinners are priced from A$12.50 in the restaurant, and the pub serves A$6 country meals.) The **Empire Hotel**, Camp and High streets (tel. 28-1030), has a similar setup with adequate rooms for A$20 single, A$40 double.

Aside from Tanswell's, you can dine well over the counter at any of the town's four pubs. There's a Chinese restaurant, the **Chinese Village**, on Camp Street, and many travelers enjoy **Rosemary's Coffee Shop** on Ford Street.

BEECHWORTH TO MELBOURNE

After a morning tour of Beechworth, you'll visit the
Brown Brothers Winery at Milawa and stop in at
Glenrowan, where Ned Kelly—Australia's most notorious
nineteenth-century bushranger—made his "last stand."
The afternoon's highlight is the Sir Colin McKenzie
Wildlife Sanctuary, an open-air reserve at Healesville that
is the best of its kind in the world. Arrive in Melbourne
in time for dinner.

Suggested Schedule	
8:00 a.m.	Breakfast in Beechworth, then explore the town and museum until about 10:30.
11:00 a.m.	Tour Brown Brothers Winery and sample the product.
11:45 a.m.	Dive into "Kelly Country" at the museums and roadside display in Glenrowan.
12:30 p.m.	Grab picnic fixings in Benalla and enjoy them on the banks of Lake Nillahcootie.
3:00 p.m.	Stroll for two hours among native Australian wildlife at the Sir Colin McKenzie Wildlife Sanctuary at Healesville.
6:30 p.m.	Arrive in Melbourne. Check into your hotel and head for a well-earned dinner on Lygon Street.

Beechworth Sightseeing Highlights
No fewer than 32 of Beechworth's buildings have been
classified or recorded by the National Trust. The best
place to start your exploration is the ▲▲ **Burke
Memorial Museum**, on Loch Street one-half block north
of Camp Street. Established at this site in 1863, it is one
of Australia's finest small-town museums. The collection
is especially strong in pioneer history, the gold rush era,
and memorabilia of the local Chinese community and the

Kelly Gang. A new gallery reproduces a 16-shop main
street of the mid-1800s with retail shops, a doctor's office,
an assay office, a dance hall, and other establishments.
Open 2:00 to 4:30 p.m. Monday, 11:00 a.m. to 4:30 p.m.
Friday, 9:00 a.m. to 4:30 p.m. all other days. (For the
sake of our tour, the Friday hours will hopefully be
extended to 9:00 a.m. as well.) Admission is A$2.

On leaving the Burke Museum, pick up a copy of the
lithographed brochure, "Beechworth Living History." Its
map will direct you to 34 points of interest in the
Beechworth area, most of them within easy walking distance. Among the properties administered by the
National Trust are the **Carriage Museum**, in the old railway depot on Albert Road, with an extensive collection
of carriages and other turn-of-the-century vehicles, and
the **Powder Magazine**, on Gorge Street at the west end
of Camp Street, a fully restored brick building where
gunpowder was cached for goldfield blasting in the
1850s. Both are open 10:00 a.m. to 12:30 p.m. and 1:30
to 4:30 p.m. daily except Friday most of the year.

Other buildings of special interest include the **H.M.
Training Prison**, the brewery museum in the old **M.B.
Cellars**, and the **Chinese Burning Towers** at
Beechworth Cemetery. If time allows, stop into the
Buckland Gallery, perhaps the most interesting of sev-
eral crafts shops in town.

The Route South

Milawa is little more than a crossroads on a secondary
route midway between Beechworth and Glenrowan. But
it's the site of one of Australia's finest wineries, the
Brown Brothers Vineyard and Winery. John Francis
Brown planted the first vines here in 1889, and four succeeding generations of Browns have carefully tended
them. Sample some of the fermented grape juice—the
cabernet and shiraz in red and the chardonnay and fron-
tignac in white are particularly good—and take a bottle
or two along for Melbourne's BYO restaurants.

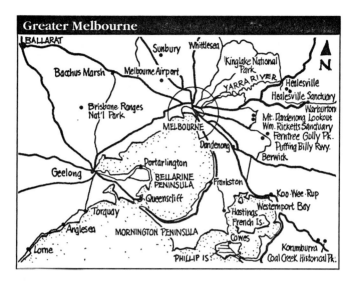

▲ Glenrowan is 21 km (13 mi.) due west. Here, in 1880, an infamous 25-year-old outlaw named Ned Kelly and his three-man gang were cornered by police at the Glenrowan Inn. Kelly's companions, including his brother, were killed in a shootout; Ned himself was wounded and brought to trial in Melbourne, where he was hanged.

Over a period of fewer than three years before his capture, Kelly had cemented a reputation as a larcenous murderer. Yet his exploits—he was a superb horseman who wore a 97-pound hand-molded suit of armor to protect himself—so fascinated Australians of past and present that he has been immortalized in poems, plays, paintings, and even a movie starring Mick Jagger.

You can't miss Glenrowan's Kelly kitsch, even if you want to. A Paul Bunyanesque statue of Ned himself, garbed in his armor and toting a rifle, holds up a train emerging from a tunnel beside the Hume Highway. The so-called Glenrowan Tourist Centre contains the Ned Kelly Sound and Visual Museum, which has a fully animated gunfight half-hourly from 10:00 a.m. to 4:00 p.m. daily (admission A$8); next door is a re-creation of the cabin that Ned and his family called home; and everywhere you look there are Kelly T-shirts, books, records, cassette tapes, mugs, keychains, pennants, and everything else imaginable. I can only advise you to keep your pennies in your pocket when you stop.

If you pause for groceries another 24 km (15 mi.) down the road at **Benalla**, famous for its rose gardens from late October through March, you can take your picnic basket to **Lake Nillahcootie**, an oasis at the foot of Mount Samaria some 40 km (25 mi.) south of town via the Midland Highway. After lunch, bypass Mansfield and pick up the Maroondah Highway, crossing the northern arm of serpentine Lake Eildon and continuing to charming Alexandra, the majestic Cathedral Range, and magnificent Maroondah fern forest. You'll arrive at the town of **Healesville** about 175 km (109 mi.) from your picnic stop.

But don't stop in town. Follow the signs another 5 km southeast to the ▲▲▲ **Sir Colin McKenzie Wildlife Sanctuary**, often known simply as the "Healesville Sanctuary." This 79-acre reserve is home to nearly 2,000 mammals, birds, and reptiles of 200 species, all of them Australian natives. Few are behind bars, and visitors have the opportunity to stroll freely through kangaroo enclosures and parrot aviaries. You'll find everything from koalas to platypuses, wombats to Tasmanian devils, emus to lyrebirds. The sanctuary is open 9:00 a.m. to 5:00 p.m. every day of the year (arrive before 3:30 if you want to see the platypus); admission is reasonable at A$7.50. A restaurant and gift shop are on the grounds. I consider the sanctuary—established in 1921 in this natural bushland setting—to be Australia's best wildlife park. Others apparently agree, for it is the most visited attraction in the state of Victoria.

If you stay at the sanctuary until the closing hour, you'll avoid most of the rush-hour traffic (it will be coming toward you, instead of with you) as you drive the final 62 km (40 mi.) west to Melbourne. Just stay on the Maroondah Highway all the way into the city.

Melbourne Orientation

A stately and sophisticated metropolis of 3 million people, Melbourne (pronounced "Melb'n," not "Mel-born") is Australia's second city. Its elegant Victorian buildings and large Mediterranean and Asian population combine to give it a cosmopolitan Old World atmosphere. It's no accident that Melbourne is the shopping, dining, entertainment, and sporting capital of the country.

Melbourne's role as Australia's financial center had more practical roots. Never a penal settlement, it was founded in 1835 by Europeans seeking to escape the more restrictive conditions on Tasmania. When the Victorian goldfields boomed in the 1850s, Melbourne became the center through which the riches were shipped. With their newfound wealth, Melbournians endowed their city with broad boulevards, beautiful parks, and classically handsome architecture. And although Sydney, with its superior harbor and 50-year head start, was the country's best-known city, it was Melbourne that became Australia's first national capital (1901-1927) and the host of its only Olympic Games (1956).

With a latitude of 38 degrees south, about the same distance from the equator as San Francisco is north, Melbourne has four distinct seasons—sometimes all in one day. Generalizations can be made—temperatures on summer days often range in the 80s Fahrenheit, while winter days average in the mid-50s—but the weather is definitely fickle, especially in the autumn months.

Melbourne's core is a neatly planned 1-by-2 km grid on the north bank of the Yarra River, with nine parallel streets running north-south and an equal number (five main streets and four widened alleys) crossing them from east to west. Swanston Street, which continues south across the Yarra, and Elizabeth Street, which connects to the Sydney–Canberra and Ballarat–Adelaide roads, are the main north-south thoroughfares. They are intersected by Flinders Street, flanking the river and the main metropolitan railway station; Collins Street, the address of most banks; Bourke Street, known for its shopping west of Swanston Street and its Chinatown east; Lonsdale Street, part of it called the Greek Precinct; and Latrobe Street, which extends east via Victoria Parade toward Healesville and the Dandenongs. You'll enter the city by this latter route.

City Transportation

The Metropolitan Transit System, known as **The Met** (tel. 617-0900), comprising rail and tram services, is Australia's best public transportation network. The trains stop at 235 stations within about a 40-km (25-mi.) radius of the city center, and the web of electric trams (the only ones in Australia) fills in the gaps that the trains neglect. It seems as though you're never more than two blocks away from one. The system runs from 5:20 a.m. to 12:30 a.m. Monday through Saturday, 6:35 a.m. to 11:45 p.m. on Sunday. Single-ride tickets within the "Inner Neighbourhood"—which includes almost all tourist attractions of note—are A$1.30; an unlimited travel three-hour ticket is A$1.90; and an all-day ticket is A$3.40. You can buy these and other tickets, as well as get free maps and more complete transit information, at Met depots, railway stations, the **Met Shop**, 103 Elizabeth Street, and the Royal Arcade kiosk between Bourke and Little Collins streets.

A new and integral part of The Met is the Melbourne Underground Rail Loop, a A$400 million project linking five stations around the perimeter of the central city.

There's also the double-decker **Melbourne Explorer Bus**, which runs every hour, 10:00 a.m. to 4:00 p.m. daily, in a loop past major tourist attractions. Tickets are A$14. You can join the bus at the Flinders Street station on the hour, and enjoy free on-and-off privileges at any of its stops.

Melbourne's international and main domestic airport is at Tullamarine, 22 km (14 miles) northwest of the city center. It is served by taxis (A$24) and by Skybus coach (A$8.50) to and from downtown hotels.

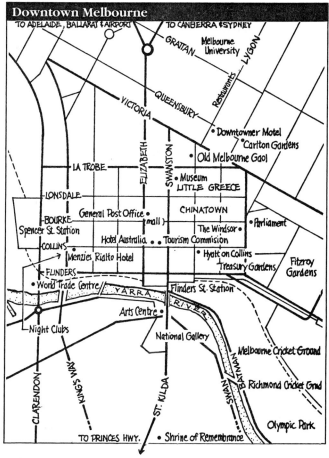

Downtown Melbourne

TO ADELAIDE, BALLARAT & AIRPORT   TO CANBERRA & SYDNEY
GRATTAN   Melbourne University   LYGON
QUEENSBURY   VICTORIA   Restaurants
• Downtowner Motel
• Carlton Gardens
LA TROBE   ELIZABETH   SWANSTON   • Old Melbourne Gaol
• Museum   LITTLE GREECE
LONSDALE
General Post Office •   CHINATOWN
BOURKE   (mall)   The Windsor •   • Parliament
Spencer St. Station   Hotel Australia •• Tourism Commission
COLLINS
→ Menzies, Rialto Hotel   • Hyatt on Collins   Fitzroy Gardens
FLINDERS   Treasury Gardens
• World Trade Centre   Flinders St. Station
Night Clubs   YARRA   RIVER
Arts Centre •
National Gallery   Melbourne Cricket Ground
CLARENDON   KINGS WAY   ST. KILDA   SWAN   BATMAN   Richmond Cricket Grnd
Olympic Park
TO PRINCES HWY.   • Shrine of Remembrance

Where to Stay

At the top of the line, Melbourne has two outstanding
hotels that eschew modern steel and concrete for the
classic look: **Le Meridien Melbourne**, 495 Collins Street
(tel. 620-9111), and **The Windsor**, 103 Spring Street (tel.
653-0653). Le Meridien has created an atrium out of two
neo-Gothic nineteenth-century buildings, while The
Windsor, opposite the old Parliament House, has
retained its century-old feeling right down to the stained-
glass dome lights in the dining room. Both cost A$290
and up.

In the moderate price bracket, the **Sheraton Hotel**, 13
Spring Street (tel. 650-5000), is centrally located opposite
Treasury Gardens; rooms start at $145. On the north side,
the **Downtowner Motel**, 66 Lygon Street, Carlton (tel.
663-5555), is close to Melbourne's best restaurant strip. A
double is A$100. Two excellent options in East
Melbourne are the charming **Magnolia Court**, 101
Powlett Street (tel. 419-4222), facing Fitzroy Gardens, and
the **Albert Heights Apartments**, 83 Albert Street (tel.
419-0955), with one-bedroom kitchen suites; rates at both
start around A$80.

In the economy class, try the **Kingscourt Motor Inn**,
15 Acland Street, St. Kilda (tel. 534-0673), with rooms
starting at A$48; or the **John Spencer**, 44 Spencer Street,
downtown (tel. 629-6991), where rates start as low as
A$36. For budget travelers, there are several **YHA youth
hostels** in North Melbourne, 3 km from downtown. The
largest, at 76 Chapman Street (tel. 328-3595), charges
A$20 a head for its 50 double rooms. The new **Queens-
berry Hill Hostel**, 78 Howard Street (tel. 329-8599), is
somewhat nearer downtown; it has dorm beds for A$17 a
night, private rooms from A$50. There are several private
hostels downtown, with beds from A$12 to A$14, including the **Backpackers City Inn**, 197 Bourke Street (tel.
650-4379). South of downtown, in St. Kilda, the **Enfield
House**, 2 Enfield St. (tel. 534-8159), is in the same price
range. You can also find good accommodations year-
round at the University of Melbourne's **International
House**, 241 Royal Parade, Parkville (tel. 347-6655), about
4 km north of downtown, with single rooms and shared
baths.

Where to Eat
Melbourne is an epicure's delight, a city with a multitude
of excellent restaurants to appeal to any palate . . . and
any wallet. This is partly a response to its attitude of self-
importance but perhaps even more a result of its broad
base of ethnic diversity. The Greeks (only Athens and
Thessalonika have larger Greek populations than

Melbourne), Italians, Yugoslavs, Turks, Lebanese, Chinese, and Vietnamese, in particular, have left their marks on Melbourne's dining habits.

There are several restaurant "strips" in Melbourne but perhaps none so acclaimed as Lygon Street in Carlton, a short stroll up Russell Street from the city center. The main Italian neighborhood of Melbourne, this is the place for pasta and pizzas. **Toto's** (No. 101), **Casa di Iorio** (No. 141), **Papa Gino's** (No. 221), and **Tiamo's** (No. 303) are among the best known, all serving good meals for less than A$12 per person. But this district is no longer strictly Italian; check Lygon and its side streets for Mexican food at **Cha Chi's**, 161 Nicholson Street; the cuisine of India's west coast at **Amritas**, 174 Rathdowne Street; Malay food at **Nyonya**, 191 Lygon Street; Caribbean cuisine at the **Jamaica House**, 106 Lygon Street; vegetarian cuisine at **Shakahari**, 329 Lygon Street.

Melbourne's most famous restaurant, **Mietta's**, is downtown near the deluxe international hotels—at 7 Alfred Place (between Exhibition and Russell streets off Collins Street). Put out A$100 for two, and you'll get an exquisite continental dinner with equally generous service. But you can eat well in the city center without breaking your budget. You can't go wrong in Chinatown (Little Bourke Street east of Swanston) if you check out the menus in the windows and see where the locals are eating. I like the **Bamboo House**, 47 Little Bourke Street, for Mandarin cuisine and the **Empress of China**, 120 Little Bourke Street, for Cantonese.

The Greek restaurants on Lonsdale Street east of Swanston are also excellent. Try **Stalactites**, Lonsdale and Russell streets, for 24-hour service, or **Tsindos The Greek's**, 197 Lonsdale Street, for Greek dancing and ritual weekend plate smashing. You'll find even more Greek eateries—plus a slew of Vietnamese places—in the Richmond district east of the city center. Similarly, there's a Turkish dining strip on Sydney Road in Brunswick, north of downtown.

A personal favorite for a splurge is **Percy's**, 384 Punt Road, South Yarra, an innovative BYO spot with a blackboard menu that changes daily. Other local choices include **Nyala** (Ethiopian), 113 Brunswick Street, Fitzroy; **Cafe Swe-Dish** (Swedish), 510 Elizabeth Street, downtown; **Sukhothai** (Thai), 234 Johnston Street, Fitzroy; and **Isabella's**, a bistro at Russell and Little Collins streets downtown.

For lunch, **Jimmy Watson's Wine Bar**, 333 Lygon Street, is hard to beat for good, cheap cuisine in an amiable atmosphere. On the south side, the **Feedwell Cafe**, 95 Greville Street in Prahran, has full meals in the A$5 range.

With some 2,000 restaurants in Melbourne, there's never a fear about where to eat. So sophisticated is the city in its dining habits that there's a white-linen restaurant aboard a tram and another on a double-decker bus!

Helpful Hints

The **Royal Automobile Club of Victoria** (RACV) (tel. 650-1522) handles tourist information on Melbourne city as well as Victoria. It is centrally located at 230 Collins Street and is open 9:00 a.m. to 5:00 p.m. Monday through Friday, 9:00 a.m. to 12:00 noon Saturday. There is also a **Melbourne Tourism Authority** (tel. 654-2288) on level 5, 114 Flinders Street.

The **Central Post Office**, at the corner of Bourke and Elizabeth streets, is open 8:00 a.m. to 6:00 p.m. Monday through Friday. Most city **banks** are open 9:30 a.m. to 4:00 p.m. Monday through Thursday, 9:30 a.m. to 5:00 p.m. Friday. Shop hours vary, but you can generally expect downtown merchants to be open from 9:00 a.m. to 5:30 p.m. Monday through Thursday, 9:00 a.m. to 9:00 p.m. Friday, 9:00 a.m. to 5:00 p.m. Saturday.

There's an **American Consulate** in South Melbourne at 24 Albert Road (tel. 697-7900) and a **Canadian Consulate** downtown at 1 Collins Street (tel. 654-1433).

In case of emergencies, dial 000.

MELBOURNE

Explore the city today. Wander through ethnic neighborhoods, sophisticated shopping arcades, and the highbrow
banking district. The Old Gaol and the National Museum
of Victoria are worthy stops. Don't miss the beautiful
Victorian Arts Centre or the nation's best botanic gardens.
But don't overdo the sightseeing. Here in sports-crazy
Melbourne, try to soak up some local culture by attend-
ing (depending on the season) a "footie" (Australian rules
football) match, cricket test, or horse race.

Suggested Schedule

9:00 a.m.	A good way to see Melbourne is to start at the north end of downtown and work your way south on Swanston Street. First stop is Queen Victoria Market, where rows of fresh fruit vendors can supply a juicy breakfast.
10:00 a.m.	The Old Melbourne Gaol and Penal Museum.
10:45 a.m.	The National Museum of Victoria, last resting place of Phar Lap.
11:45 a.m.	Explore the Greek Precinct and Chinatown, stopping in one or the other for lunch.
1:00 p.m.	Bourke Street Mall and shopping arcades.
2:00 p.m.	Collins Street, Melbourne's "Golden Mile."
2:30 p.m.	Victorian Arts Centre, the largest multiarts complex in the world.
3:30 p.m.	The National Gallery of Victoria, Australia's finest art museum.
5:00 p.m.	Royal Botanic Gardens.
6:00 p.m.	Dinner.
7:00 p.m.	Join the fanatic throngs at a sports event. There's always something on Saturday night.
10:00 p.m.	Climax your day with a little nightlife.

Sightseeing Highlights

▲**Queen Victoria Market** is a large, open-air market near the intersection of Queen and Victoria streets. (The main entrance is off Franklin Street.) On Tuesday, Thursday, Friday, and Saturday mornings starting at 6:00 a.m., it's a multicultural potpourri of fruit and vegetable vendors, while on Sundays from 9:00 a.m. to 4:00 p.m., it turns into an enormous flea market especially popular among craft and antique dealers. There are more than 1,000 stalls.

▲▲**The Old Melbourne Gaol and Penal Museum**, Russell Street near Lygon, is a dank and morbid but fascinating relic of the days (1841 to 1929) when men were men and felons were hanged. Here are the gallows and isolation cells known and feared by hundreds of convicts, including the notorious bushranger Ned Kelly. The jail exhibits Kelly's handmade armor and his "death mask," created for phrenologists to study possible clues to his deviant behavior. Open 9:30 a.m. to 4:30 p.m. daily except Sunday. Admission A$5.50.

▲▲**The National Museum of Victoria**, Swanston and LaTrobe streets, has an excellent exhibit of state history, a new science and technology section, plus good natural history and ethnography displays. Deep within its chambers, however, is the reason so many Australians consider this a religious shrine. Phar Lap, generally regarded as the greatest racehorse that ever lived, stands within a glass display case. The steed won an incredible 37 of his 51 starts, earning over A$133,000, before dying a mysterious death in Menlo Park, California, in 1932 at the age of 5. (If you saw the 1983 Australian movie *Phar Lap*, you know all this.) The museum is open daily from 10:00 a.m. to 5:00 p.m. Free admission.

The Greek Precinct of Lonsdale Street, from Swanston to Russell Street, has been upgraded to emphasize the outdoor cafés and colorful specialty shops. The traditional Edwardian character of the buildings has been maintained. If you're here in March or April, chances are you'll catch a festival.

▲**Chinatown**—two blocks from Swanston Street to
Exhibition Street, bisected by Little Bourke Street—is
linked to the Greek Precinct via Heffernan Lane. Chinese
have lived in this neighborhood since 1854. The opium
dens have long since closed, but many of the butchers,
bakers, and candlemakers still ply trades learned from
their forefathers. Today, the restaurants and shops on
Little Bourke and its side lanes, especially Celestial
Avenue, comprise the most interesting Chinatown in the
Southern Hemisphere. The **Museum of Chinese
Australian History**, 22 Cohen Place, contains photographs, artifacts, and an audiovisual presentation. Open
Sunday to Thursday 12:00 noon to 5:00 p.m. Admission
A$3.

▲**Bourke Street Mall** is the shopping center of
Australia's shopping capital. The Myer Emporium, for
example, is the world's second largest department store
(after Marshall Field's in Chicago), taking up a good portion of two city blocks on the north side of the mall.
Next door to it is David Jones, Australia's answer to J. C.
Penney. The south side of the mall is interlaced by a
maze of delightfully restored shopping arcades. In particular, check out the Royal Arcade, with its campy 1892
clock depicting Gog and Magog striking the time.

There are several other great shopping streets in the suburbs. Armadale High Street is packed with antique, craft,
book, and clothing shops; Chapel Street and Toorak
Road are the hubs of a glitzy high-fashion neighborhood
in South Yarra; and St. Kilda's Acland Street is famous for
its pastry shops

Parliament House, on Spring Street at the east end of
Bourke, was built in 1856 and served as the federal
Parliament until the provisional house in Canberra
opened in 1927. It still serves as Victoria's state assembly
chambers. Guided tours are offered at 10:00 a.m., 11:00
a.m., 2:00 p.m., and 3:00 p.m. Monday through Friday.

▲**Collins Street** is where the nation's most important
financial institutions are housed, many of them in

Victorian gold rush masterpieces spliced between steel-
and-glass skyscrapers. If you're here on a weekday, take
a walking tour, starting at the **ANZ Banking Museum**
(open 9:30 a.m. to 4:00 p.m. Monday through Friday) in
the basement of the Australia-New Zealand Bank, 386
Collins Street. Then step inside the institution upstairs for
a look around, and also have a peek into the Bank of
New Zealand (No. 395), National Australian Bank (No.
335), and WestPac (No. 331). The **Melbourne Stock
Exchange**, 351 Collins Street, has a third-floor visitors
gallery with a broad view of the trading floor. It's open
Monday through Friday from 9:00 a.m. to 12:00 noon and
2:00 p.m. to 5:00 p.m.

▲▲**The Victorian Arts Centre** is modern Melbourne's
pride and joy. The city proudly trumpets that this is "the
largest arts center in the world." Indeed, the complex—
completed in 1985—includes a 2,600-seat concert hall,
three theaters for opera, ballet, and drama, three licensed
restaurants, an art shop, a museum, and the adjoining
National Gallery of Victoria. Its 500-foot Eiffel-like spire,
which towers over the Yarra River beside St. Kilda Road,
can be seen for miles around.

A variety of tours are offered to show off the Centre
and its unusual architecture. There are morning and after-
noon tea tours weekdays for A$23, or luncheon tours for
A$43. Evening tours, starting promptly at 5:00 p.m.
Monday through Friday, include dinner and a play for
A$57. Short tours at 12:00 noon and 2:30 p.m., daily except
Saturday, cost A$4. Sunday backstage tours are A$9.

The Melbourne Symphony Orchestra often plays free
lunchtime concerts, and every Friday from 5:00 to 7:00
p.m., there's a free jazz show in the basement Monsanto
Lounge. Bookings should be made for all other performances and tours by calling 684-8484 or 684-8151.

▲**The Performing Arts Museum** in the concert hall is
highly regarded internationally. Its changing exhibits
range from silent films or horror movies to re-creations of
Dame Nellie Melba's operatic recordings. Open 11:00

a.m. to 5:00 p.m. Monday through Friday, 12:00 noon to
5:00 p.m. weekends. Admission is A$4.

▲▲▲**The National Gallery of Victoria**, on the south
side of the Victorian Arts Centre at 180 St. Kilda Road,
was Australia's first public art gallery (founded in 1861)
and is still the finest in the Southern Hemisphere. Its
most popular galleries to overseas visitors are those of
Aboriginal and Oceanic art and of Australian art, especially featuring its noted Heidelberg school of late
nineteenth-century impressionists—Tom Roberts, Arthur
Streeton, Frederick McCubbin, and Charles Condon. Its
collection of more than 50,000 works also includes divi-
sions of European, British, and American art, Asian art,
pre-Columbian art, costumes and textiles, decorative arts,
prints and drawings, and photography. Open daily
except Monday from 10:00 a.m. to 5:00 p.m. Admission
A$3.

▲▲**The Royal Botanic Gardens**, a half-kilometer stroll
south and east of the Arts Centre, is considered one of
the world's best landscaped gardens. More than 12,000
plant species thrive in the 88 acres of lawns, garden
beds, and ornamental lakes, along with over 50 species
of birds. It's open 7:00 a.m. to sunset daily.

Adjacent to the gardens is the much larger **King's
Domain**, containing the massive **Shrine of
Remembrance** war memorial; the circa-1840 **La Trobe's
Cottage**, Victoria's original government house (open
Monday and Wednesday 10:00 a.m. to 4:00 p.m., week-
ends 11:00 a.m. to 4:00 p.m., admission A$3.50; and the
Sidney Myer Music Bown, an outdoor amphitheater in
summer, a covered public ice rink in winter. The 11-km
Yarra River Bikeway starts here; bicycles can be hired
opposite the Botanic Gardens in Alexandria Avenue from
11:00 a.m. to dusk weekends and holidays.

Melbourne's other famous parks include **Fitzroy
Gardens** in East Melbourne between Wellington Parade
and Albert Street. Its highlight is **Captain Cook's
Cottage**, transported here from Yorkshire, England, in

1934 and reassembled (open 9:00 a.m. to 5:00 p.m. daily, admission A$2). The adjacent **Treasury Gardens**, facing Spring Street, contain a John Kennedy memorial. **Carlton Gardens**, Victoria Street opposite Spring, contains the Royal Exhibition Buildings built in 1880 for the inauguration of the Commonwealth of Australia. **Albert Park**, between South Melbourne and St. Kilda, has a large lake with boat rentals.

▲**The Royal Melbourne Zoo**, on Elliott Avenue in Royal Park (north of the city center), is the third oldest zoo on Earth. The aviary, they say, is bigger than Paris's Cathedral of Notre Dame. The 55 acres have recently been relandscaped, with most of the 336 species now in simulated natural environments. Open 9:00 a.m. to 5:00 p.m. daily. Admission A$9.

▲**Como House** (1855), on Como Avenue in South Yarra, and ▲ **Ripponlea** (1887), at 192 Hotham Street in Elsternwick, are two beautiful colonial mansions set in spacious suburban gardens. Both have been refurnished with the trappings of the Victorian elite; both are open daily 10:00 a.m. to 5:00 p.m. and charge A$5.50 admission. (Ripponlea has limited winter hours.)

▲**The Polly Woodside**, anchored in the Yarra River at Normanby Road and Phayer Street in South Melbourne, is a restored iron-hulled Irish sailing vessel now finding new duty as the focus of a maritime museum. Open daily 10:00 a.m. to 4:00 p.m. Admission A$7.

Sports in Melbourne

Australia in general—and Melbourne in particular—comes to a stop on the first Tuesday of November when the Melbourne Cup is run at Flemington Racecourse. In fact, this world-famous horse race is celebrated as a public holiday in Victoria. And that's indicative of the reverence with which Melbournians regard sports in general.

After all, this is where Australian rules football was invented. Victorians have set out to evangelize the world with this sport that isn't soccer, isn't rugby, certainly isn't

American football, but has elements of all three—and some of its own. Most of Australia's capital cities are now represented in the Victorian Football League, and the ESPN cable television network in the United States broadcasts a game of the week. Upwards of 100,000 fans attend major matches at the venerable Melbourne Cricket Ground. The season starts in April and concludes with the Grand Final on the last Saturday of September.

About the time "footie" is winding down, cricket is just beginning. Its season runs from October to March, concluding with the Sheffield Shield, pitting each Australian state against the others until one claims the national championship. A single test match can take five 8-hour days to play. (There are free 2-hour guided tours of the cricket ground beginning at 10:00 a.m. every Wednesday.)

Melbourne hosts many other important sports events, including the Ford Australian Open tennis tournament at the National Tennis Centre on Batman Avenue. To find out what's happening (and where) during your visit, check the sports pages of *The Age*, Australia's best newspaper.

Melbourne Nightlife

Melbourne doesn't have any equivalent to Sydney's Kings Cross. Its nightlife is spread across the metropolis, from downtown to the suburbs. St. Kilda, a short hop south of the city center, tends to be the hippest area; Richmond (east) and Carlton (north) can also be lively.

The Friday morning edition of *The Age* gives full listings of the entertainment week ahead. Rock music dominates the scene, but you'll find far more jazz and acoustic music in Melbourne than in other big cities.

The only thing approaching a downtown "strip" is King Street from Collins to Flinders. In one block, there's live rock at **Inflation** and **X**; disco at the **Hippodrome**; jazz and folk at the **Grainstore Tavern**. Nearby, on Bourke Street near Spring, is the Southern Hemisphere's largest disco (with eight bars), **Melbourne Metro**. Some of the night spots are open all night—you can rage 'til 7:00 a.m.

The **Limerick Arms Hotel**, 36 Clarendon Street, South Melbourne, and the **Tankerville Arms Hotel**, on Nicholson Street in Fitzroy, are two of the city's best venues for live jazz, while the **Moomba Hotel** in North Melbourne is good for country sounds Wednesday through Friday.

The No. 1 meeting spot in town, at this writing, was the **Hyatt on Collins**, at the corner of Russell Street. The casual bars and restaurants in the basement of its atrium are packed from the off-work hours to closing. Next door, the **Ivy Club**, Flinders Lane and Russell Street, draws actors, rock stars, and other so-called "beautiful people." The **Station Hotel**, Greville and Chapel streets in Prahran, is a brew pub that draws good crowds for rock and jazz, while the **Sherlock Holmes Inn**, 421 Collins Street, attracts lovers of traditional British pubs.

Young and Jackson's, 1 Swanston Street at Flinders, is Melbourne's most famous pub and one of its oldest. Since the Melbourne Exhibition of 1880, it has displayed above its bar an oil painting of "Chloe"—a full-length nude that once shocked Victorian sentiments.

For symphony, theater, opera, and ballet, the obvious first choice is the **Victorian Arts Centre** (see Sightseeing Highlights). Other major stages downtown—**Her Majesty's Theatre**, 219 Exhibition Street, and the **Princess Theatre**, 163 Spring Street—are within three blocks of each other. This section of downtown Melbourne, along Bourke Street between Spring and Swanston, is also the location of most cinema houses for first-run movies.

Melbourne hosts two major festivals during the year. Moomba, in March, is the Mardi Gras Down Under. Gian Carlo Menotti's Spoleto Arts Festival, in September/October, is a more sedate but culturally fulfilling event.

BALLARAT

Ballarat is synonymous with two subjects near and dear to Australians' hearts: gold and independence. Today's outing covers both ends of this historic Victorian city— Sovereign Hill, the country's No. 1 theme park, faithful to its 1850s heyday; and the Eureka Stockade, site (in 1854) of a much-heralded rebellion unique in Australian history.

Suggested Schedule

8:00 a.m. Leave Melbourne, heading west on the Great Western Freeway (Highway 8).

10:00 a.m. Arrive in Ballarat. Sovereign Hill is the town's central attraction. Plan to spend several hours, including lunch.

2:00 p.m. Cross the street to the Gold Museum.

3:00 p.m. Relive the glory of the Eureka Stockade.

4:00 p.m. See Montrose Cottage, the Botanic Gardens, or another of Ballarat's attractions.

5:30 p.m. Head back to Melbourne for dinner and rest.

Ballarat Orientation

Victoria's second-largest city (pop. 90,000), Ballarat is located 113 km (70 mi.) west of Melbourne. It was founded by gold-diggers in 1851 and quickly became an Eldorado, with fortune hunters from around the world converging on the settlement after hearing fairy tales about gold nuggets being plucked off the streets. In fact, the argonauts had to work for their gold, but they pulled an estimated 20 million ounces from the hills before the last mine closed in 1918. At today's prices, that would be worth about US$7 billion.

Much of that money that gold wrought was poured into constructing a beautiful town on the frontier. With the opening of the railroad in 1862, Ballarat became the gateway to western Victoria, and its future was assured. Today, it is known for its gardens and art galleries as much as for its historic sites. The Western Highway—Sturt Street through most of downtown—bisects Ballarat into northern and southern halves. **Ballarat Tourism**, 39 Sturt Street (tel. 053/32-2694), is in the center of town. Sovereign Hill is perhaps a mile south of the center on Bradshaw Street (just off Main Road). The Eureka Stockade, exhibition, and diorama are on Stawell Street, just south of the Western Highway at the east end of Ballarat.

City Transportation

If you don't drive to Ballarat—if you perchance took the train or bus to Melbourne—you can shuttle to the town's attractions on **Clarks Shuttlebus** (tel. 35-9770). Seven loop trips a day are operated around the city, taking in Sovereign Hill and the Eureka Stockade. You can board at the railway station, disembark, and reboard wherever you choose along the route for A$8. The Shuttlebus also travels between Ballarat and Melbourne's Tullamarine Airport three or four times daily, with A$40 covering roundtrip transportation plus admission charges at Sovereign Hill and the Eureka exhibition.

Sightseeing Highlights

▲▲▲**Sovereign Hill** is a place of living history, an authentic re-creation of Australia's most important gold mining township of the 1850s. Operated by a nonprofit local association whose 200 volunteers dress in period costume, the park has three main sections. In the Red Hill Gully Diggings (faithful to the period 1851-1855), brightly dressed miners emerge from their tents and mud huts to show visitors how to pan for alluvial gold. In the Goldmining Township (1854-1861), horse-drawn coaches roll past 29 separate working businesses—among them a blacksmith, coachbuilder, tinsmith, confectioner, printer, potter, and furniture maker with a steam-driven lathe. In

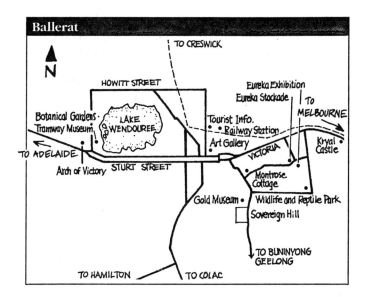

the Mining Museum (1860-1918), you can travel underground to learn how quartz reef mining was done, while above you a thunderous stamper battery crushes the gold-bearing quartz.

Main Street is Sovereign Hill's core. You can dine in style at the New York Bakery or the licensed United States Hotel. (Takeaway food and barbecue supplies are also available in the Township.) You can attend comedy sketches in the Victoria Theatre, or try your hand at skittles in the Empire Bowling Saloon.

Low-cost accommodations are available at Government Camp, a re-created 1850s military barracks on a hill overlooking the Township. Though the buildings might appear old, they're comfortably modern within. Families can stay for A$55 a night (for four); there's also a YHA youth hostel on the site. The park is open daily (except Christmas) from 9:30 a.m. to 5:00 p.m. Admission is A$15; for A$38, you can get a Gold Pass, which includes a coach ride and admission to the adjacent Gold Museum.

▲▲**The Gold Museum**, on Bradshaw Street across from the Sovereign Hill car park, is a worthy adjunct to the theme park. Its historical exhibits, while emphasizing the gold rush era and Eureka Stockade rebellion, also recall central Victoria's Aboriginal history and the creation of its wool industry. The Gold Pavilion displays important private collections of rare gold coins from around the world and turn-of-the-century Chinese artifacts. Open 9:30 a.m. to 5:30 p.m. daily except Christmas. Admission A$3.

▲▲**Eureka Stockade** is a name with the same ring to Australians as the Alamo has to Texans. Like Davy Crockett and Jim Bowie et al., the miners lost this battle. But they won the war.

Mercilessly taxed and oppressed by the British colonial administration, the diggers made a gallant stand for their democratic rights. The climax came on December 3, 1854, when government troopers attacked a stockaded position held by miners near the Eureka diggings. Six troopers and 22 miners died. The tragedy shocked Victoria's colonial leaders into introducing long-awaited reforms in the goldfields. Within a year, two leaders of the revolt were elected to the first Victorian Parliament under a new constitution.

Today, at the Eureka Street Parkland (at the corner of Stawell Street), the rebellion is remembered by a memorial, a reconstructed stockade, and a diorama of the incident. More impressive is the **Eureka Exhibition**, catty-corner from the memorial at Eureka and Kline streets, with a series of computer-controlled scenes depicting various episodes of the revolt. Open daily 9:00 a.m. to 5:00 p.m.; admission A$3.

The miners' famous Southern Cross banner flew over the stockade for only five days—yet Aussies hold it in the same esteem as Americans do Betsy Ross's "13 stars on a field of blue." The Eureka flag can be seen in the **Ballarat Fine Art Gallery**, 40 Lydiard Street. The gallery is open Tuesday to Friday, 10:30 a.m. to 4:30 p.m., Saturday and Sunday, 12:30 p.m. to 4:30 p.m.; admission is $2.

▲**Montrose Cottage**, 111 Eureka Street, is the earliest original bluestone masonry cottage surviving from 1850s Ballarat. Classified by the National Trust, it contains the small Eureka Museum of Social History. Open daily 9:30 a.m. to 5:00 p.m.; admission A$4.

The Botanic Gardens encompass 100 acres around Lake Wendouree on the northwest side of Ballarat. Prime Ministers Avenue, within the gardens, is flanked by bronze busts of all Australian prime ministers, right up through the leader in 1993, Paul Keating.

Kryal Castle, 8 km east of Ballarat on the Western Highway, is a curiosity: a re-created medieval castle where costumed actors reenact the life and pageantry of the Middle Ages. There's jousting, sword-fighting, even the occasional hanging, and a tavern where a medieval banquet is held every Saturday night. Open 9:30 a.m. to 5:00 p.m. daily except Christmas. Admission is A$9.50.

Golda's World of Dolls, 148 Eureka Street, displays more than 2,000 rare antique and period-costumed dolls from all over the world. Open 1:00 to 5:00 p.m. daily except Friday.

The Arch of Victory, at the west end of Ballarat, marks the beginning of the tree-lined, 21-km Avenue of Honour dedicated to the men and women of Ballarat who volunteered for active service abroad during World War I.

DANDENONG RANGES AND PHILLIP ISLAND

The "Blue Dandenongs," a relaxing day trip on the east side of Melbourne, contain many beautiful gardens, a unique sculpture forest, a park noted for its lyrebirds, and various other attractions. The day's highlight comes at dusk, when hundreds or thousands of tiny fairy penguins parade from the sea to their burrows up a concrete walkway, as hundreds of cameras click away.

Suggested Schedule	
9:00 a.m.	Leave Melbourne right after rush hour.
10:15 a.m.	Stroll through the William Ricketts Sanctuary, with its environmentally oriented sculptures of Aboriginal Mother Nature.
11:00 a.m.	Visit Mount Dandenong Observatory to gaze at the high-rises of Melbourne in the distance.
11:30 a.m.	The artisans' village of Olinda is also the site of the National Rhododendron Gardens.
12:15 p.m.	Lunchtime at an Olinda or Sassafras tearoom.
1:00 p.m.	The elusive lyrebird runs free in Sherbrooke Forest Park.
2:00 p.m.	Take a quick swim at Emerald Lake Park or visit a model railway museum near the terminus of the Puffing Billy steam train from Belgrave.
4:30 p.m.	Arrive at Phillip Island for the penguin parade. The parade occurs about dusk, so the exact time varies from season to season.
After Dark	Return to Melbourne, stopping for dinner en route.
(Note: On Sundays, these roads are always packed by local day-trippers. Plan to skip a couple of attractions in the Dandenongs to reach Phillip Island on time.)	

The Dandenong Ranges

The forested mountains east of Melbourne aren't especially high—Mount Dandenong itself is only 633 meters
(2,076 ft.)—but enough to lift them above the occasional
smog of Port Phillip Bay and endow them with a rich
plant and animal life. A surprising number of artists and
nature lovers choose to live in the Dandenongs and com-
mute 60 to 90 minutes (each way) daily to the city.

The fastest route to the Dandenong Ranges is to head
back east on the Maroondah Highway as though going to
Healesville, but turn right at Ringwood on the well-
marked Mount Dandenong Road. A drive of about an
hour from the city brings you to Montrose at the northern
end of the Mount Dandenong Tourist Road Sightseeing
highlights of the Dandenongs, moving down the road
from north to south, include:

▲▲**William Ricketts Sanctuary**—Like J. R. R. Tolkien
gone mad, Ricketts (born in 1899) is an eccentric musi-
cian-turned-artist-turned-environmental radical. His
enchanting clay sculptures decorate a lovely fern forest
on the slopes of Mount Dandenong; indeed, they are a
part of the forest, carefully melded to existing trees,
rocks, and brooks. All of Ricketts's work has Aboriginal
and spiritual overtones. His more recent sculptures also
make fierce animal rights and antiexploitation statements.
"Being part of nature," he writes, "we are brothers to the
birds and trees. Will you then join with us in the sacred-
ness of beauty?" Open 10:00 a.m. to 4:30 p.m. daily.
Admission A$4.

▲**Mount Dandenong Observatory**—Outside the moun-
taintop restaurant and tearoom are a roadside observa-
tion area and a handful of coin-in-the-slot telescopes to
gaze across at the metropolis of Melbourne in the near
west.

Edward Henty Cottage—A pioneer museum and
antique shop occupy the former home of one of the
Dandenongs' early residents. It is located a short distance
above Olinda. Admission to the museum is A$1.50.

▲**Olinda**—Art galleries and small restaurants specializing in midday Devonshire teas line the road around this picturesque village. It's worth getting out of the car and walking around.

▲**Sherbrooke Forest Park**—Take any of the tranquil trails through this lush nature preserve and you're likely to see or hear the lyrebird, a grouse-sized ground bird with a long, lacy, peacocklike tail used in courtship demonstrations. The lyrebird is remarkable for its ability to mimic almost any sound it hears, from other birds to machinery. (I was once awakened while camping by the sound of a logging truck. There were no logging roads nearby, but there were lyrebirds.) Also in the forest are Sherbrooke Falls, Alfred Nicholas Memorial Gardens, and four picnic grounds with barbecue facilities.

Fern Tree Gully National Park—Just above the town of Upper Ferntree Gully, this small park encompassing a valley of beautiful tree ferns offers pleasant walks and colorful rosellas galore.

Belgrave—Another artists' community, somewhat larger than Olinda, Belgrave lies at a major junction in the Dandenongs. It's best known as the depot for Puffing Billy.

▲▲**Puffing Billy**—Australia's best-known narrow-gauge steam railroad, built in 1900 to carry farm produce, packs its wooden cars with weekend and holiday day-trippers year-round, daily during school vacations (except on days of total fire ban). Puffing Billy typically leaves Belgrave at 10:30 a.m. on its 13-km (8-mi.), 40-minute run up and down the ridges to Emerald Lake Park, returning at 12:40 p.m. There are additional runs on weekends. Round-trip fare is A$11.50 for adults, A$7.70 for children. (Call 870-8411 for timetable specifics.) There's a **Steam Museum** at Menzies Creek, open 11:00 a.m. to 5:00 p.m. Sundays and holidays, with a collection of early locomotives. We won't have time for a ride on Puffing Billy on this itinerary, but you may enjoy it if you have an extra day or two in Melbourne.

▲**Emerald Lake Park**—A spacious, well-kept park surrounding a lake popular with swimmers and fishermen, this is the eastern terminus of Puffing Billy. Above the station is a pavilion containing Australia's largest model railway: over 2 kilometers of track. A youth hostel stands near the park's entrance. In Emerald village are many quaint shops and craft galleries.

Phillip Island

It will take about 30 minutes to drive from Emerald Lake Park to Pakenham and another 90 minutes to follow the South Gippsland and Bass highways south to San Remo, at the east end of the 604-meter (2,100-foot) Narrows Bridge connecting Phillip Island to the Victoria mainland.

Phillip Island's main attraction—one of the outstanding sights in all of Australia—is the ▲▲▲ **Penguin Parade** at Summerland Beach, near the island's southwestern tip, every night of the year. A colony of fairy penguins numbering in the thousands spend most of their days fishing in Bass Strait, returning at dusk to their burrows in the sand dunes at this protected reserve. Bright lights illuminate the beach as the penguins straggle in to land and under cleverly constructed boardwalks, while a crowd of camera-happy tourists quietly views the penguins from above. These little (foot-high) birds are so cuddly looking that it's hard not to smile as you watch them waddle through their nightly ritual, apparently oblivious to all the human attention. Flash cameras are not permitted.

You can buy tickets to the viewing area (for A$6) at the Penguin Reserve office beginning an hour before the parade or at the Phillip Island Information Centre near San Remo, open daily 9:00 a.m. to 5:00 p.m. Book ahead by credit card by calling (059) 56-8300 or 56-7447. Entrance tickets include admission to a multimillion-dollar visitor information center, well worth inspecting before or after the parade.

The penguins aren't the only wild denizens of 25,000-acre Phillip Island. Koalas may be seen in the eucalyptus groves of **Oswin Roberts Reserve** or the **Five Ways Koala Reserve**. Fur seals maintain an offshore colony on **The Nobbies**, a 50-million-year-old volcanic rock stack: up to 4,500 of the marine mammals breed here in November and December. Mutton birds (short-tailed shearwaters) nest on Cape Woolamai, the island's southeasternmost point.

The island also features a dairy, a shell museum, a center for wool artisans, three chicory kilns, a historic homestead on Churchill Island (connected to Phillip Island by a footbridge at Newhaven), a small wildlife park, a large blowhole, a cavern, a golf course, and other standard resort amenities.

Cowes, the island's main town (on the north shore), has ample accommodations and eating places. (In summer, it's best to dine before the parade, because the restaurants close early.)

MELBOURNE TO ALICE SPRINGS

Drop your car at Melbourne's Tullamarine Airport and catch a morning flight to Alice Springs. You'll have all afternoon and evening to explore this outback oasis. Visit the Old Telegraph Station and the Royal Flying Doctor Service. To climax your day, ride a camel down the dry Todd River bed to dinner at a desert winery.

Suggested Schedule

6:45 a.m.	Return car to Tullamarine Airport.
7:50 a.m.	Depart Melbourne on Australian Flight 22 for Alice Springs.
11:15 a.m.	Arrive at Alice Springs.
12:00 noon	Check into your accommodation. Lunch.
1:00 p.m.	Orient yourself at the Anzac Hill viewpoint.
1:30 p.m.	See the Old Telegraph Station.
2:30 p.m.	Visit the School of the Air.
3:00 p.m.	Drop in on the Royal Flying Doctor Service.
4:00 p.m.	Take a camel to dinner.
9:00 p.m.	Return to Alice Springs.

Leaving Melbourne
Flemington Road leads north into the Calder Highway, taking you to Melbourne International Airport at Tullamarine. Arrive well before your flight departure to turn in your rental car.

Alice Springs Orientation
With a rapidly growing population of about 25,000, "The Alice" is the biggest town for more than 800 miles in any direction. A desert oasis, it is situated in the midst of the MacDonnell Ranges, almost exactly in the geographic center of the continent. Australians call this area "The Centre" (or "The Red Centre" because of the unusual color of its soil).

Founded in 1872 as a station on the Overland Telegraph Line between Adelaide and Darwin, it got its name when stationmaster Charles Todd dubbed a permanent waterhole in the bed of the usually dry Todd River "Alice Springs" after his wife. When the railroad came through in 1929, the population was still only 200. A road from Adelaide was completed about 1940; only in 1987 was the final link paved. The population didn't reach 1,000 until the 1950s or 5,000 until the 1970s. Modern tourism, however, has contributed to a boom throughout the Northern Territory, especially in The Alice.

The central business district is a compact 12 square blocks between the highway and the Todd River, bounded by Wills Terrace on the north and Stott Terrace on the south. The Todd Street Mall, a pedestrians-only thoroughfare, stretches for two blocks from Gregory Terrace to Wills Terrace a block west of the river and is regarded as the center of town. It is bisected by Parsons Street and is paralleled to the west by Hartley and Bath streets and to the east by Leichhardt Terrace overlooking the river.

The word "river," by the way, is a misnomer. To be called a "local" in Alice Springs, one must have seen the Todd flow its length three times. Some 20-year residents are still waiting to become locals. The river is completely dry most of the year.

The **Northern Territory Government Tourist Bureau**, Ford Plaza at Todd Mall (tel. 52-1299), has a wide selection of maps, brochures, and other information, including detailed walking and driving tours of the city area.

City Transportation

Alice Springs Airport is some 13 km (8 miles) south of the city center. Pay A$7 for shuttle service up the Stuart Highway to downtown.

There's no public transportation in Alice Springs except for taxis, and they're rather expensive. If you want to get out and see the town—beyond what you can easily walk to—you have these options:

1. Hop aboard **The Alice Wanderer**. This bus visits the town's major attractions on an hourly circuit; you can visit one site, reboard an hour later, and hop off at the next attractions. Tickets are A$15 all day, A$10 for a half-day.

2. Rent a car for the day. You can get an open "moke" for as little as A$20 a day and 20 cents a km, plus $10 for insurance. (That's a cost of A$40 if you do 50 km of driving.) A compact will run A$30 a day and 20 cents a km.

3. Hire a car and driver, at a rate of A$40 for two hours. The Northern Territory Government Tourist Bureau has a list of operators.

4. Join a bus tour. Three-hour tours operated by AAT Kings, among others, are priced at A$35, including all admissions.

5. Rent a bicycle or moped. Thrifty Bike Hire on Todd Street has bikes for A$10 for an 8-hour day, mopeds for A$25 a day. The tourist bureau can tell you about other locations.

Sightseeing Highlights

Anzac Hill, named in honor of the combined World War I and II armed forces of Australia and New Zealand, offers a good view of Alice Springs and the surrounding terrain. Drive the circular road off Stuart Highway, or hike the steep Lions Walk from the end of Bath Street off Wills Terrace.

▲▲**The Old Telegraph Station** is 3 km north of Alice Springs off the Stuart Highway. The reserve has restored the original 1872 telegraph station and equipment and displays early photographs and historical documents. There are nature walks and a small wildlife park nearby, as well as a picnic ground and barbecue area beside the Alice Springs waterhole. Open 8:00 a.m. to 9:00 p.m. October to April, 8:00 a.m. to 7:00 p.m. the rest of the year. Admission A$2.50.

▲**The School of the Air** provides education by short-wave radio to children through the Central Australian outback, some as far as 1,000 km (621 miles) away. Visitors are invited to observe and listen between 1:30 and 3:30 p.m. on school days (Monday through Friday except holidays). Adult admission is A$1. The school is located beside Braitling School in Head Street, about 1½ miles north of downtown.

▲▲**The Royal Flying Doctor Service** was established in 1939 by the Rev. John Flynn, probably The Alice's best-known historical figure, to deliver medical attention to isolated homesteads by small plane. Today it relies more on radio communication to serve thousands of square miles from New South Wales and Queensland to Western Australia. Tours of the base, near the south end of Bath Street on Stuart Terrace, are offered every half hour from 9:00 to 3:30 p.m. Monday through Saturday, and from 1:00 to 4:00 p.m. Sunday. Admission is A$2.50. (Flynn's original aircraft is on display at the Aviation Museum on Memorial Drive, at the old Alice Springs airport.)

▲**Panorama Guth**, 65 Hartley Street north of Stott Terrace, is the private gallery of painter Henk Guth, who has created an unusual 360-degree mural of the terrain surrounding Alice Springs. Guth also has a collection of photographs, Aboriginal artifacts, and watercolor paintings of the Hermannsburg School. Open 9:00 a.m. to 5:00 p.m. Monday through Friday, 9:00 a.m. to 12:00 noon and 2:00 to 5:00 p.m. Saturday, 2:00 to 5:00 p.m. Sunday. Admission is A$3.

▲**Pitchi Richi Sanctuary**, on Aranda Terrace south of Heavitree Gap near the Todd River causeway, combines William Ricketts' unique Aboriginal-theme sculpture with an outdoor folk museum and wild bird refuge. If you missed the Ricketts Sanctuary in the Dandenong Ranges east of Melbourne, don't miss this. Open Monday to Saturday 9:00 a.m. to 5:00 p.m., Sunday 10:00 a.m. to 4:00 p.m. Admission is A$3.

▲**Diorama Village**, 2 km west of downtown on Larapinta Drive at Bradshaw Drive, uses narrated dioramas to depict Aboriginal myths—like how the kangaroo got his tail and how the Milky Way was formed. Open 10:00 a.m. to 5:00 p.m. daily; admission is A$3.

▲**Strehlow Research Centre**, also on Larapinta Drive, preserves Australia's largest collection of Aboriginal spirit objects, entrusted to the late Professor Ted Strehlow during his 40 years of work with the Aranda people. While these items are not on public display, the Centre presents a state-of-the-art computer-controlled exhibit on Strehlow's studies of the Aranda; the building itself has the largest compacted-earth wall south of the Equator. Open daily 10:00 a.m. to 5:00 p.m. Admission is A$4.

▲**Aboriginal art galleries** exhibit and sell the arts and crafts of the native tribes of Central Australia—the Arunta, the Curindji, and the Pitjantjatjara. Browse at the government-operated Centre for Aboriginal Artists and Craftsmen, 86 Todd Street, or any of a dozen other shops and galleries.

Frontier Camel Farm, 4 km south of town on Emily Gap Road (the Ross Highway), is open for riding these "ships of the desert" from 9:00 a.m. to 5:00 p.m. daily. It also has a Magic Spark Museum of early radio communications. Admission is A$6.50.

The Mecca Date Garden on Emily Gap Road is Australia's only commercial date garden, with 20 varieties of productive date palms. Open daily 9:00 a.m. to 5:00 p.m. (It's closed November through January.) Admission, including a conducted tour, is A$1.50.

▲**The Henley-on-Todd Regatta** is perhaps the most exciting boating race never to take place on water. Every year on the last weekend of September, 40-foot yachts line up in the dry riverbed, gripped tightly on the gunwales by their crews, who run with them as fast as they can. It's a good excuse for a party.

Where to Stay

The top of the line in Alice Springs is represented by the modern **Sheraton Alice Springs**, Barrett Drive (tel. 089/52-8000), with doubles over A$200. A notch down is the **Four Seasons Alice Springs**, Stephens Road (tel. 52-6100), with prices ranging to about A$130. Both are on the south side of town. Centrally located and moderately priced are the **Elkira Motel**, 65 Bath Street (tel. 52-1222); the **Desert Rose Inn**, 15 Railway Terrace (tel. 52-1411); and the **Oasis Frontier Resort**, 10 Gap Road at Traeger Avenue (tel. 52-1444), all in the A$80 range for two.

For economy lodging, try **The Old Alice Inn**, 1 Todd Mall (tel. 52-1255), with rooms for A$35. The YWCA's **Stuart Lodge**, Stuart Terrace near Todd Street (tel. 52-1894), takes both men and women for A$25 single, $35 double. The **Melanka Lodge**, 94 Todd Street (tel. 52-2233), has private rooms around A$55, and wearing its other hat—as the **Alice Springs Backpackers Lodge**—offers dorm beds from A$11. Two **YHA Hostels**, one at Todd Street and Stott Terrace (tel. 52-5016), a newer one on Parsons at Leichhardt Terrace (tel. 52-8855), offer dorm beds for A$10 to $12.

Where to Eat

Aside from hotel coffee shops and restaurants, there is a good variety of dining establishments in Alice Springs. Steak and spicy food lovers appreciate **Overlander Steakhouse**, 72 Hartley Street, with meals in the A$12 to A$15 range. Ask for buffalo steak in witchety grub sauce. The Old Alice Inn, at the corner of Todd Street Mall and Wills Terrace, has the popular **Maxim's**, with continental cuisine under A$10 including an all-you-can-eat vegetable bar. For Italian food, try the licensed **La Casalinga**, 105 Gregory Terrace. **Chopsticks**, in the Ermond Arcade on Hartley Street, is the local Chinese favorite with Cantonese and Szechuan cuisine. Good, cheap breakfasts and lunches cost no more than A$6 at the **Eranova Cafeteria**, 72 Todd Street.

Fifteen km (9½ mi.) south of Alice Springs is **Chateau Hornsby**, Central Australia's first and only winery. The wine isn't great, but it's certainly palatable—and dry! There's an informal outdoor barbecue area, fine for lunches, and a pleasant indoor restaurant, where local bus balladeer Ted Egan performs most nights. Find it at the end of Petrick Road, off Colonel Rose Drive.

On Sundays, Tuesdays, Wednesdays, and Fridays, for A$65, you can **"Take a Camel to Dinner"** by joining Frontier Tours' sundown safari down the Todd River bed to Chateau Hornsby. The price includes an hour on a camel's back and a five-course barramundi (fish) or buffalo roast dinner. The beasts leave Alice Springs at 4:00 p.m. (returning at 9:00 p.m.) October through April, departing at 3:00 p.m. May through September. You can also take a camel to breakfast or lunch, incidentally. Book at your hotel or call 53-0444.

Nightlife

Alice Springs isn't Sydney or Melbourne. But it does have a casino. **Lasseter's Casino** on Barrett Drive, on the southeast side of town, is named after Harold Lasseter, a local legend who perished in the desert searching for a fabled reef of gold in 1931. Harry should have lived so long; the gold is here, on the gaming tables. The casino also has a disco open Thursday 11:00 p.m. to 4:00 a.m., Friday and Saturday 11:00 p.m. to 5:00 a.m.

There's live music Thursday through Sunday at the **Old Alice Inn**, Wills Terrace and Todd Street Mall, and the **Stuart Arms Hotel**, Parsons Street and Todd Street Mall. **Bojangles Nightclub**, Todd Street near Stott Terrace, is open nightly except Sunday for meals and disco dancing 'til the wee hours.

If there's more upscale entertainment in town, you'll find it at the **Araluen Arts Centre**, west of downtown on Larapinta Drive. The Alice's center for the performing and visual arts attracts name entertainers from Australia and overseas.

ALICE SPRINGS TO AYERS ROCK

Marvel at the weird geology of the Red Centre as you fly from Alice Springs to Yulara resort village at Ayers Rock, arriving in the early afternoon. After getting settled in your lodging and exploring the community, sip champagne as you watch the sun set over the red rock.

Suggested Schedule	
9:00 a.m.	You'll have time to do some shopping or sightseeing in Alice Springs before taking a shuttle bus to the airport.
12:20 p.m.	Australian Flight 56 for Ayers Rock.
1:00 p.m.	Arrive at Ayers Rock's Connellan Airport.
1:30 p.m.	Get settled in your accommodations, take a dip in the pool, eat lunch, then drop by the Yulara Visitors Centre and tour the resort complex.
Open	Go to the Sheraton lookout tower 45 minutes before sunset to sip champagne and watch the Rock's colors change. Then dinner.
9:00 p.m.	Early bedtime for tomorrow's "ordeal."

Ayers Rock Orientation

The great red monolith of Ayers Rock is the symbol of the Australian outback, at once an irresistible spiritual force to the Aboriginal people and a testimony to the stark, primeval beauty of the desert landscape.

There is no larger rock on earth. Yet Ayers Rock may not be as well known for its massive size (1,260 feet high, 5 miles around its base) as for its moods. From dawn to dusk, the Rock undergoes a continuous series of subtle color changes, from sunrise pink to midday brown, sunset red to post-sunset purple. During the rare desert downpours, it can even appear silvery with rain cascading down its time-sculpted slopes.

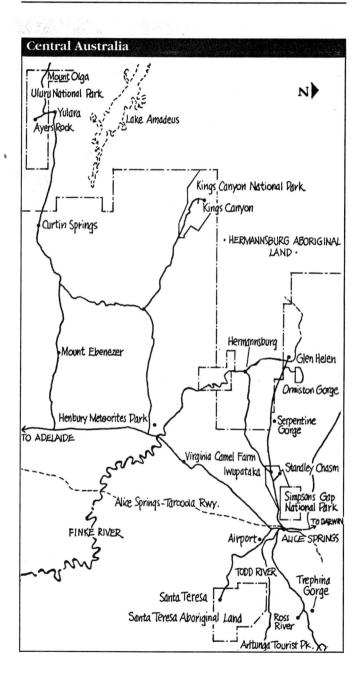

Central Australia

Mount Olga
Uluru National Park
Yulara
Ayers Rock
Lake Amadeus

N▶

Kings Canyon National Park
Kings Canyon

Curtin Springs

• HERMANNSBURG ABORIGINAL
LAND •

Mount Ebenezer

Hermannsburg

Glen Helen
Ormiston Gorge

Henbury Meteorites Park

TO ADELAIDE

Serpentine
Gorge

Virginia Camel Farm
Iwupataka

Standley Chasm

Alice Springs-Tarcoola Rwy.

Simpsons Gap
National Park

TO DARWIN

FINKE RIVER

Airport •

ALICE SPRINGS

TODD RIVER

Trephina
Gorge

Santa Teresa

Santa Teresa Aboriginal Land

Ross
River

Arltunga Tourist Pk.

The ancient Loritja and Pitjantjatjara tribes called the Rock "Uluru." Thousands of years ago, they decorated the cave walls around its base with paintings and petroglyphs. Not until 1872 did Europeans know of the Rock; Ernest Giles sighted it during his explorations of the Centre, and the following year, William Gosse led a three-month camel caravan to climb the monolith. Today, the ascent is a relatively simple, if strenuous, morning excursion.

About 510 square miles surrounding Ayers Rock and the nearby Olgas Range—piled high like a giant's marbles above the sandy earth—were established in 1958 as Ayers Rock-Mount Olga National Park. Title for the parklands was transferred to the Aboriginal people in 1985, and Uluru National Park came into being. Commercial enterprise—motels, a campground, and an airstrip—was moved out of the shadow of the Rock.

Yulara, 19 km (12 mi.) from Ayers Rock, was built to provide comfort in the desert sun for the rapidly growing influx of tourists. Only 2,300 people visited Ayers Rock when the national park first opened in 1958; but by 1990, with a sealed, 468-km (291-mi.) all-weather road linking the Rock to Alice Springs, Uluru was attracting 220,000 visitors from all over the world—despite being one of the costliest destinations in Australia.

The resort village, completed in 1984, can accommodate up to 5,000 people a day in two luxury hotels, two midpriced hotels, a lodge, and a spacious campground. And it is a complete village—in fact, with its resident population of around 500, it is the third largest community in the sparsely settled Northern Territory (after Darwin and Alice Springs). There's a small shopping square, a school, a medical center, a community hall and sports center, a police station, and other facilities to keep the people from feeling too isolated.

Still, they must cope with the summer heat and year-round temperature extremes. From December to February, daytime temperatures average about 97 degrees Fahrenheit, dropping to around 70 at night; mid-winter temperatures range from average daytime highs of 58 to nighttime lows of 41, though freezing temperatures are not uncommon. Total rainfall is only 10 inches a year, with February the wettest month (1.5 inches) and September the driest (.25 inch).

Yulara Transportation

There isn't any cheap way to get around here, short of walking. The shuttle bus for the short hop from the airport to Yulara costs A$7 one way; the price of the three-times-a-day shuttle from the resort to Ayers Rock is A$20 round-trip, or a little under $1 a mile. And so it goes. AAT Kings and Bus Australia share the concession. Some visitors find the three-day "Rock Pass," allowing unlimited trips on the shuttle buses to the Rock and the Olgas, a worthwhile purchase at A$47.

Cars are available for rent, but they're hardly a bargain. If the weather cooperates—and it usually does—consider hiring a moped from the Mobil Service Station in Yulara village. Half-day (four-hour) rental is A$25, full-day A$40.

Where to Stay

The **Sheraton Ayers Rock Hotel** (tel. 089/56-2200) is the luxury leader, with 230 rooms rambling around a lovely swimming pool and courtyard. Twin rooms are A$260 a night. Many visitors prefer the A$180 rooms across the village at the **Four Seasons Ayers Rock Motel** (tel. 56-2100). More moderately priced are the **Yulara Mansionettes** (tel. 56-2131), with A$95 twins. The **Red Centre Hotel** (tel. 56-2170) has rooms at A$165, cabins at A$78, and dorms for large parties (A$20 a bed). There are also 20 on-site vans in the **Ayers Rock Campground** (tel. 56-2170), available at A$60 a night for two.

Where to Eat

The **Sheraton** has two fine restaurants, the **Four Seasons** another. At either hotel, you can get a filling

buffet dinner for around A$25. There are three less
expensive options, perhaps the best being the counter
meals and buffet at the **Ernest Giles Tavern**, open
daily in the Shopping Square. The adjacent **Old Oak
Tree Coffee Shop** has light meals and takeaways, while
the **Red Centre Hotel** is popular for its casual home
cooking.

AYERS ROCK

If the world's largest monolith is awesome at sunset, it's even more stunning at dawn. Awaken early to watch the spectacle and to beat the heat and flies as you scale the huge red rock. Then you too can wear a T-shirt declaring, "I climbed Ayers Rock." Visit the craft exhibit at the Uluru National Park ranger station and search for ancient petroglyphs in caves around the base of Ayers Rock. Later, join a sunset tour to The Olgas.

Suggested Schedule

6:45 a.m.	Leave Yulara via shuttle bus for Ayers Rock.
7:30 a.m.	Begin climb up Ayers Rock. Allow at least 90 minutes for the round trip.
9:00 a.m.	Tour base of rock by bus, take the ranger-guided hike to Kantju Gorge, or stroll to Maggie Springs.
11:45 a.m.	Visit the ranger station to see the outdoor exhibit of Aboriginal crafts and video.
12:45 p.m.	Back to Yulara aboard shuttle bus.
1:30 p.m.	Lunch, swim, relax.
Time varies	Join a sunset barbecue tour to The Olgas.
9:00 p.m.	Listen to the bush band at the Sheraton, or call it an early evening.

Sightseeing Highlights
▲▲▲**Climbing Ayers Rock** is a must, as long as you're in reasonably good physical condition. The ever-cautious national park administration warns that the average time of climbing the 1.6 km (1 mile) to the cairn and returning to the foot of the Rock is two hours. As a slightly out-of-shape, over-the-hill hiker, I can accomplish it in a little over an hour, including 15 minutes or so relaxing and taking photos at the top. But don't push yourself too hard; if you feel exhausted or nauseous, quit. Take a break, then head back down.

The first 500 meters of the climb are the steepest. A staunch chain has been sunk into the Rock to provide a handhold for any and all who need it while ascending the 45- to 60-degree angle. Once that portion has been surmounted, it's merely an uphill walk, with just a couple of precipitous drops and rises across eroded ridges.

At the top, you'll be rewarded with an unfettered view of hundreds of miles of red dirt. Be sure to sign the climbers' register, noting the vast array of nationalities who have put their home address there next to your own. After a short rest, you can head back down. Your calves got a workout on the way up; now your thighs will feel it. Some climbers find it easier to back down the chain on the steepest stretch.

The best shoes for climbing are rubber soled. Any kind of athletic shoes work as well as proper climbing boots. Don't go in street shoes, thongs, or bare feet. Bring something with you to drink, and if you're starting much later than 8:00 a.m., put on suntan lotion and a sun hat. The wind can be stiff, so be sure to tie down anything you carry—or it may wind up at the bottom of the Rock long before you do.

▲**Circling the Rock** aboard the shuttle bus can be done if you're back at the base by 9:00 a.m. The driver-guide points out Taputji (Little Ayers Rock), Maggie Springs, and other sites around the Rock's circumference en route back to Yulara. It's interesting to note how different Ayers Rock appears from different viewpoints. The tour costs A$26, including the shuttle fee from Yulara.

▲**Ranger-guided walks**, which leave at 9:00 and 10:00 a.m. from the car park at the base of the Rock climb, are free. For over an hour, hikers accompany a park ranger into Kantju Gorge, a cleft in the Rock with an adjacent waterhole. The ranger explains Ayers Rock's place in Aboriginal legend and tells about the geology and environment of this Central Australian region.

▲▲**Maggie Springs**, known to the Pitjantjatjara as "Mutitjulu," is a deep, tranquil pool nestled against the southeast wall of Ayers Rock. After a rainstorm, you can often see tiny desert frogs and fairy shrimp in the water. The hideaway is especially striking in the late morning, when the blue of the outback sky contrasts sharply with the red of the rock and the green of the mulga and desert oak vegetation. Nearby are several small caves, their walls and roofs adorned with Aboriginal cave paintings thousands of years old. Maggie Springs is a level 2-km walk from the shuttle bus stop.

▲**Uluru National Park Ranger Station**, where everyone who enters the park is supposed to stop and pay a A$10 use fee (valid for three days), has a number of exhibits of special interest to the park visitor. In particular, take some time to talk with the native Mutitjulu people who display the works of Aboriginal artists and craftspersons in an outdoor gallery adjoining the ranger station.

▲▲**The Olgas**, to many visitors, are even more spectacular than Ayers Rock itself. An accumulation of 36 oddly shaped domes that rise from the Central Australian desert some 32 km (20 miles) west of the Rock, they were known to the Aboriginals as "Katatjuta" and feared as hungry giants. Indeed, the Olgas can be sirens who lure explorers into their seductive wonderland only to cook them alive in a midday oven. Every year, it seems, unbelieving foreign visitors perish in the Olgas. By late afternoon, the heat is off again. There are afternoon and evening tours of these mountains—the latter including a barbecue dinner at sunset—for prices starting at A$29.

Nightlife

A bush band performs Aussie sing-along and dance music most nights in the Sheraton's **Mulgara Bar**. It's good fun, the best reason to visit the Sheraton if you're not staying there. The **Ernest Giles Tavern** has a pub disco several nights of the week.

AYERS ROCK TO KINGS CANYON

Learn about the Aboriginal culture today. Spend the morning with a native guide who will show you how her people found food, water, shelter, and medicine in this arid landscape. After lunch, board a bus for the 175-mile drive to Kings Canyon Frontier Lodge.

Suggested Schedule

8:30 a.m.	Join the "Liru Walk" with an Aboriginal guide from the Uluru Ranger Station.
11:30 a.m.	Lunch at Yulara.
1:30 p.m.	Farewell to Ayers Rock.
4:00 p.m.	Rest stop at Angas Downs turnoff.
7:00 p.m.	Arrive Kings Canyon Frontier Lodge for overnight stay.

Sightseeing Highlights

▲▲**The Liru Walk** happens only three times a week, but it's worth catching when it does. Beginning at 8:30 a.m., Mondays, Wednesdays, and Fridays, an Aboriginal woman (females are the traditional food-gatherers in Central Australia) leads a group from the Uluru National Park Ranger Station on a two-hour bush walk to demonstrate how her people survived in this arid climate using only natural food sources. You'll learn, for instance, that the burrowing witchety grub is superb food, 50% protein and 50% fat; that the fruit of the plumbush tree has the highest known concentration of vitamin C; that the prolific mulga tree has seeds that can be ground to make flour; and that the flowers of the hakea tree, mixed with water, make a drink similar to cola. And remember that scene in *Crocodile Dundee* where Mick skewers a large lizard for dinner? Your guide will show you where to find a tasty sand goanna just like it.

In fact, there is a bewildering variety of wildlife here in the desert. Naturalists have counted 290 species of plant life, 151 birds, 52 reptiles, and 22 native mammals. The most prolific of all creatures is the blowfly, sort of a larger, more persistent version of the American housefly. Out of direct sunlight and with a bit of a breeze, you'll find they're not bad. In most other circumstances, they're extremely unpleasant. You'll soon learn why "The Great Australian Salute" is a hand waving past your face to keep these flies out of your eyes, ears, nose, and throat.

Flies notwithstanding, the Liru Walk is a fascinating look at a life-style very different from our own. The A$10 charge includes bus transport from Yulara, and tour numbers are limited, so book ahead by phoning 56-2240.

▲▲**Ayers Rock-Kings Canyon tours** are conducted by several tour companies based in Alice Springs. Any Northern Territory Government Tourist Bureau can provide a complete listing. You can hook into a luxury coach tour through AAT Kings Tours (about A$150 a day; 74 Todd Street, Alice Springs, NT 0870, tel. 089/52-5266), or a budget camping trip offered by Sahara Outback Tours (about A$80 a day; 118 Bloomfield St., Alice Springs, NT 0870; tel. 089/53-0881). Both have frequent (though not daily) departures on the three-day Alice–Ayers Rock–Kings Canyon–Alice circuit. The trick is to join a tour in progress on departure from Yulara. Advance arrangements are essential.

You'll leave Yulara on the Lasseter Highway, a 247-km (153-mile) thoroughfare connecting Ayers Rock with the Stuart Highway, the main north-south route from Adelaide to Darwin. About 138 km (86 miles) from Yulara, following a rest stop at the Curtin Springs homestead and a view of isolated Mount Connor, you'll turn north past Angas Downs to Kings Canyon, 189 km (117 miles) farther.

The **Kings Canyon Frontier Lodge** has 100 motel units, a bunkhouse, caravan park, and camping area, with economy and moderate prices. It's just 7 km from Kings Canyon itself. Full restaurant services are also offered.

KINGS CANYON TO ALICE SPRINGS

Wander between the sheer walls of colorful Kings Canyon, then return to Alice Springs in the evening. If you're not totally exhausted, enjoy a nightcap at the casino.

Suggested Schedule	
7:00 a.m.	Rise and shine; eat breakfast.
8:00 a.m.	Leave for Kings Canyon.
8:30 a.m.	Explore the spectacular chasm. Wander through the lush Garden of Eden and climb to the canyon rim for marvelous panoramic views.
11:30 a.m.	Leave Kings Canyon.
12:00 noon	Lunch at the Frontier Lodge.
1:30 p.m.	Leave for Alice Springs.
4:30 p.m.	See the Henbury Craters.
6:00 p.m.	Arrive at Alice Springs for the night.

Sightseeing Highlights
▲▲▲**Kings Canyon**, Australia's spectacular "grand canyon," is a deep cleft in the George Gill Ranges, about 250 km (155 air mi.) southwest of Alice Springs.

Sheer sandstone walls rising 700 to 900 feet above the canyon floor vary in hue from pink to crimson, ivory to deep purple. In the Garden of Eden, lush palms grow around dozens of waterholes, reflecting the multicolored walls like so many kaleidoscopes. In the Lost City, rocky outcrops look like primitive rock dwellings of a forgotten tribe. The Sphinx is another formation unique in this terrain. You may find rock wallabies and goanna lizards at the waterholes, and you'll certainly see rose-tinted galahs and a variety of other birds. It's a steep climb to the canyon rim—more difficult than the struggle up Ayers Rock—but the panoramic views from the summit make the climb worthwhile. As at the Rock, you should wear rubber-soled shoes for climbing, apply suntan lotion, wear a sun hat, and carry something to drink.

Kings Canyon road runs the 198 km (123 mi.) from the canyon to the Stuart Highway. The road has recently been paved. If you're driving your own vehicle, watch out for road flooding, particularly where it crosses the Palmer River. This arid land doesn't absorb rainfall quickly, so even a half inch of precipitation can have a major effect on road conditions. Beware of collisions with kangaroos, wild camels, and brumbies (wild horses). Carry water—at least a gallon per person per day of your trip—plus reserve gas, a tool kit, two spare tires, and extra engine parts. It helps if you have a mechanical inclination.

▲**Henbury Craters** are an odd cluster of about a dozen meteor craters off Kings Canyon Road near its junction with the Stuart Highway, 132 km (82 mi.) south of Alice Springs. Between 2,000 and 3,000 years ago, a shower of meteorites rained down on this 40-acre conservation park, creating craters from 20 to 600 feet across and as much as 50 feet deep. A walking trail from the car park signposts many of the features.

▲**The Virginia Camel Farm**, 90 km (56 mi.) south of The Alice, is Noel Fullerton's contribution to Central Australian culture. Fullerton originated Alice Springs' Lions Club's "Camel Cup" in the 1970s, won it himself four times, and subsequently placed his teenage children in the championship category of camel riding. (The Cup races are held annually in May.) The farm domesticates some of the Centre's estimated 30,000 wild camels and breeds others for export to—of all places—the Arab world, from which Australia's herd originated! Visitors can pay a few dollars for a short camel ride or book a one- or two-week safari east into the Rainbow Valley.

ALICE SPRINGS TO CAIRNS

Today, fly from Alice Springs to Cairns. On your arrival in Cairns, the humidity will tell you immediately that you're in the tropics. Have a cold beer at an Esplanade pub, watch the fishing and pleasure boats return from the Great Barrier Reef, see the Reef World aquarium. For dinner, order barramundi, a delectable river-run cod.

Suggested Schedule	
8:30 a.m.	Leisurely breakfast at hotel.
9:30 a.m.	You've got the better part of the day for sightseeing or shopping in the Alice; then take a shuttle bus to the airport.
4:25 p.m.	Australian Flight 293 to Cairns.
7:15 p.m.	Arrive at Cairns International Airport. Take a bus 8 km to town and check into hotel.
8:30 p.m.	Dinner at one of Cairns's fine seafood eateries.

Cairns Orientation

Cairns (don't pronounce the "r") is the undeclared capital of lazy, tropical North Queensland. A rapidly growing town of about 70,000 people on the shores of Trinity Bay, it is wedged against a backdrop of rain forest-clad mountains, facing the so-called eighth wonder of the world, the Great Barrier Reef.

Founded in the mid-1870s as a customs collection point and a port for gold and tin mines in the interior of Queensland, it later grew as a center for sugarcane growing and processing. Sugar and tin remain economically important today, along with fishing, timber, and tropical fruit.

But tourism is taking over as the No. 1 revenue producer. The number of tourists coming here doubled between 1979 and 1984 and doubled again between 1984 and 1991. Some two dozen new hotels with over 4,500 rooms have been built in the greater Cairns area since 1985. The Cairns airport now has direct flight connections with nearby Papua New Guinea and the U.S. West Coast via Honolulu, as well as Tokyo, Bangkok, and Singapore, making it more accessible to tourists than ever before.

Why do the tourists come? The primary reason is the reef. No population center along the Australian coast is closer to the coral phenomenon than Cairns, with the Outer Reef a mere two-hour launch trip away. Second, they come for the fishing. Cairns is famed for its sport-fishing fleet; international celebrities use Cairns as a base for marlin fishing. Third, they come for the jungle. Some of the last great tracts of rain forest on earth are west of Cairns on the Atherton Tableland and north around Cape Tribulation.

Cairns itself is an easy town to find your way around. It's stereotypically tropical, its ornate, wide-verandaed homes often raised well above the ground for air circulation. The streets are wide and palm fringed, the harbor a bustling center of trade amid squawking seabirds. Spence Street runs due west from the marlin jetty; it's paralleled to the north by Shields, Aplin, Florence, Minnie, and Upward streets. The Esplanade, which runs along the shore from Upward to Spence, and McLeod Street, which fronts the railroad tracks, mark the eastern and western boundaries of the downtown district. Abbott, Lake, Grafton and Sheridan streets run between, from east to west. City Place, a mall marking the center of the city, is at the intersection of Shields and Lake. Sheridan Street is the main thoroughfare north toward the airport and the Cook Highway.

City Transportation
A regular shuttle bus service operates between Cairns International Airport and town, a distance of 8 km (5

miles), for A$4. (Leaving town, call 35-9555 for pickup times). Taxi fare between Cairns and the airport is about A$10.

If you arrived in Cairns by train from Brisbane or other points south, you'll disembark at Cairns Station on McLeod Street, at the end of Shields Street. All downtown points are within easy walking distance. (The economy single adult rail fare from Brisbane to Cairns, one way, was about A$113 at this writing. The "Sunlander" arrives Sunday, Tuesday, and Friday at 7:45 p.m. after a 34-hour trip; the "Queenslander" express come in once a week, at 5:55 p.m. Monday.)

A variety of bus services are available within and around Cairns at reasonable fares. (Schedules are posted in the foyer of the O.T. Corporation and on the window of Rockman's both on Shields Street between City Place and Abbott Street.) The Cairns Red Explorer charges A$18 for a full day's circuit of city attractions. The transit center for all lines is at Trinity Wharf.

Car rentals are also readily available in town and at the airport. For cheap moke or moped rentals, check with Mini Car Rentals, 150 Sheridan Street. You can rent bicycles in several locations, including Cycle Works, Aplin and Lake streets, and the Bicycle Barn, 61 Sheridan Street.

Where to Stay

With all those new hotels, and some three dozen older ones, there are a wide variety of accommodations available in Cairns. Generally speaking, you'll find the budget and moderate lodging in the town itself. Luxury hotels are often up the coast, among them **Ramada Great Barrier Reef Resort** at Palm Cove (tel. 070/55-3999), about 25 km (16 miles) north of Cairns. The A$150 million **Sheraton Mirage Resort**, 76 km (47 miles) from Cairns at Port Douglas (tel. 070/99-5888), has private villas, five acres of swimming lagoons, and an 18-hole championship golf course.

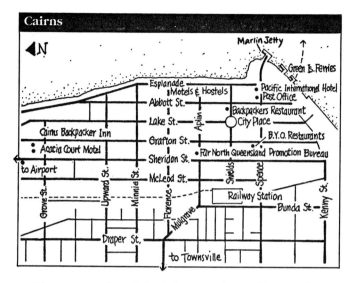

The top new hotels in Cairns are the **Radisson Plaza at the Pier**, Pier Point Road (tel. 070/31-1411), and the **Cairns International**, 17 Abbott Street (tel. 070/31-1300). Both are stunning properties.

In the moderate price class, it would be hard to do better than the **Cairns Colonial Club**, 18-26 Cannon Street (tel. 53-5111), which surmounts the minor drawback of being a couple miles north of the city center with regular free shuttle service. A choice of rooms at several price levels, starting at A$69, are nestled around an open-air restaurant-bar and saltwater pool, complete with sandy beach and waterfall. A good in-town alternative is **The Outrigger**, at Florence and Abbott streets (tel. 51-6188).

Economy travelers will do well at the **Silver Palms Private Hotel**, 153 The Esplanade (tel. 51-2059), and the **City Court Garden Apartments**, 13 Charles Street (tel. 51-7642), both equipped with kitchens. And those touring on a shoestring will quickly learn why Cairns is becoming one of the budget travel capitals of the world. The biggest of five hostels is **Caravella's**, 77-81 The Esplanade (tel. 51-2159). There are others on The

Esplanade at Nos. 67, 85, 89, and 149. A bit quieter is the
Cairns Backpackers Inn, 255 Lake Street (tel. 51-9166).

Sightseeing Highlights
▲▲**The Marlin Jetty** is a "must" stop during the sport-
fishing season, which runs from August into December.
When private boats and charter operators return here
toward evening with their days' catches, the heart of
even the veteran fisherman has to thump a little. Black
marlin, hoisted onto the scales, may go well over the
1,000-pound mark.

▲**The Cairns Museum**, located in an early twentieth-
century School of Arts building at the corner of Lake and
Shields streets, has displays of natural history, North
Queensland Aboriginal artifacts, gold mining (and early
Chinese habitation), and railway construction. Open
10:00 a.m. to 3:00 p.m. Monday through Friday.
Admission is A$1.

Blue Water Coral Factory, about 3 km from the Cairns
town center at 82 Aumuller Street, presents a workshop-
viewing area and a 10-minute video on the making of
coral jewelry. Open daily; admission is free.

Flecker Botanical Gardens, Collins Avenue in Edge
Hill, 2 miles from the town center, comprise a luxuriant
century-old tropical jungle and parkland with more than
10,000 species of trees, shrubs, and flowers. There's a
great view across Cairns to Trinity Bay from the top of
Mount Whitfield. Open daily sunrise to sunset. Admission
is free.

Where to Eat
For a relatively small city, Cairns offers an awesome vari-
ety of international cuisine in its many restaurants. Some
of the licensed seafood restaurants have the most style.
Try **Scuppers**, Grafton and Aplin streets; **Fathoms**,
Grove and Diggers streets (near Grafton), especially for
the garlic chili crab; or **Tawny's** on the Marlin Jetty. **Lin
Nam**, 14 Aplin Street, has good Chinese seafood. An

excellent BYO seafood eatery is **Avocado**, 228 Sheridan Street.

Among other BYO restaurants, these are a few of the best, by cuisine: **Der Feinschmecker** (German), 95 Grafton Street; **Toko Baru** (Indonesian), 42 Spence Street; **Omar Khayyam** (Lebanese), 82 Sheridan Street; **Bangkok Room** (Thai), Spence and McLeod Streets; **Taj** (Indian), Spence and Sheridan Streets; **Daman's** (Italian), 64 Shields Street; **Casa Gomez** (Spanish), 48 Aplin Street; and **Sweethearts** (vegetarian), in Rusty's Bazaar on Grafton Street.

Along The Esplanade and around the City Place mall, several restaurants have outdoor tables set up to catch the eyes and noses of passersby. One of the most popular for lunch is **Swagman's Rest**, in City Place.

Last, but far from least, is the **Backpackers' Restaurant** on Shields Street just east of City Place. With a name like that, its clientele is—you guessed it—mainly backpackers. And it's always packed. Counter meals are cheap and good, beer is cheap and good, and both are served into the wee hours.

Nightlife

The scene changes often in a resort town like Cairns, but at this writing, the favored upscale nightclubs were the **Playpen International**, 2 Lake Street; **Tropo's**, a disco at Lake and Spence Streets, and the **House on the Hill**, Kingsford Street in out-of-the-way Mooroobool. All are open until 3:00 in the morning, although nights of closing vary.

Close to the city center, you can enjoy a quiet drink and conversation to the music of a piano bar or light jazz at **The Nest**, 82 McLeod Street; **Duke's**, upstairs at 86 Lake Street; and **Kipling's Wine Bar**, 79 Abbott Street.

The **Jabiru** cabaret restaurant, in the Parkroyal Shopping Village, Lake Street, offers traditional Aboriginal and contemporary entertainment from 7:00 nightly.

Young rockers find loud music and cheap drinks at

the **End of the World**, Abbot and Aplin Streets. The **Crown Hotel**, 35 Shields Street, is always good for a rage. You'll often find the fishermen in **Oscar's Bar** at the Great Northern Hotel, 69 Abbott Street.

Helpful Hints

The best source of travel and touring information once you've arrived in Cairns is the **Far North Queensland Promotion Bureau**, 36-38 Aplin Street at Sheridan Street (tel. 51-3588). Open weekdays 9:00 a.m. to 5:00 p.m.

The **Central Post Office** is on the corner of Florence and Sheridan streets. **Banks** stay open from 9:30 a.m. to 4:00 p.m. Monday through Thursday, to 5:00 p.m. Friday. Retail shops in the downtown area are open 8:30 a.m. to 5:15 p.m. Monday through Thursday, to 9:00 p.m. Friday, to 12:00 noon Saturday.

In case of emergencies, dial 000.

GREAT BARRIER REEF

You'll leave Cairns this morning to spend the day snorkeling or diving on the outer Barrier Reef. It is an incredible experience to see more than 200 species of tropical reef fish swimming through an undersea "garden" of multicolored coral.

Suggested Schedule

8:30 a.m.	Leave Cairns Trinity Wharf for Michaelmas Cay and the Outer Reef.
10:45 a.m.	Arrive at Michaelmas Cay.
2:45 p.m.	Leave Michaelmas Cay.
5:00 p.m.	Return to Cairns.
6:30 p.m.	Dinner, perhaps followed by tropical nightlife.

Sightseeing Highlights

▲▲▲**The Great Barrier Reef** is truly one of the wonders of the world. Stretching for more than 2,000 km (1,250 mi.) down the coast of Queensland from New Guinea to the Tropic of Capricorn, it is the largest structure (80,000 square miles of individual reefs, shoals, and islets) ever created by living creatures.

Tiny marine animals called polyps (closely related to sea anemones) are the master engineers. Forming colonies linked by a network of tubes and protected by an external skeleton of lime, they forever grow on the mass remains of their forebears. Their formations are as varied in color as in shape, from red fans to yellow staghorn, purple "brains" to green cabbage, and many, many more.

Snorkeling or diving in the reef is like taking a swim through an underwater garden. I've put on a mask and fins in bodies of water all over the world, from Hawaii to the Indian Ocean, but never have I been more astounded than on the Barrier Reef. More than 1,400 species of fish have been identified here, each seemingly brighter and more fan-

ciful than the last. There are turtles and rays, starfish and
sea urchins, jellyfish and giant clams, and more.

The polyps' only known enemy, by the way—besides
the polluting or vandalizing human—is the crown-of-thorns
starfish. This creature is a formidable foe indeed, one pos-
ing a real challenge to marine biologists trying to control the
escalating degeneration of parts of the reef.

The best place from which to approach the underwater
wonderland of the Great Barrier Reef is right where you are
now. At its southern end, the reef is nearly 160 km (100 mi.)
from the Queensland coast near Rockhampton, and it takes
a long boat trip (or a seaplane hop) to reach it. From
Cairns, it's but a 20- to 30-km (12- to 20-mi.) trip from the
Australian mainland to the inner edge of the reef.

▲▲**Michaelmas Cay**, 45 km (28 mi.) northeast of Cairns, is
of particular note among the reef islets because it is a tern
rookery. Thousands of the squawking seabirds circle over-
head, protecting their young in their nests and squabbling
over shellfish on the isle's sands. (Visitors may carry umbrel-
las to protect themselves from smelly aerial assaults.) The
cay also has superb diving on the offshore reef.

Of various cruises to the outer reef, I recommend the
Quickcat II, a 105-foot (32-meter) twin-masted catamaran. It
leaves Trinity Wharf daily at 8:30 a.m. for Michaelmas Cay,
with a two-hour stop at Green Island. A lunch buffet
(including prawns and tropical fruit), afternoon tea, snorkeling gear, and guided narration by marine biologists are provided to all who pay the A$99 adult fare (children half-
price). Scuba diving equipment and drinks from the bar are
extra. Make reservations by calling 31-2920.

▲▲▲**Hastings Reef** lies on the reef's outer fringe, where
the coral is the youngest and the variety and color of
marine life are the greatest. Michaelmas Cay is at the edge
of this reef. Don't let cloudy weather put you off a trip to
this submarine phenomenon, 55 km (34 miles) northeast of
Cairns. For one thing, the filtration of rays through the
clouds actually brings out the reef's colors, especially the
blues.

KURANDA

The scenic Kuranda Railway will take you inland to the edge of the rain-forested Atherton Tableland, climbing steeply above fields of sugarcane to the Barron River Gorge and Barron Falls. You'll reach Kuranda in time to see the famous Tjapukai Aboriginal dance troupe perform. After lunch, see the wildlife noctarium and the butterfly sanctuary before returning to Cairns for dinner.

Suggested Schedule

7:30 a.m.	Breakfast at your hotel.
8:30 a.m.*	Depart Cairns by rail for Kuranda.
10:00 a.m.	Arrive Kuranda.
11:00 a.m.	Catch a performance of the Tjapukai Dance Theatre, a one-hour professional stage show of Aboriginal culture.
12:15 p.m.	Take time for lunch in Frogs Restaurant or the Kuranda Trading Post.
1:30 p.m.	Tour the Australian Butterfly Sanctuary.
3:00 p.m.	Visit the Kuranda Wildlife Noctarium.
4:00 p.m.	Depart Kuranda for Cairns.
5:30 p.m.	Arrive in Cairns. Return to your hotel, change, and go out for dinner.

*Cairns-Kuranda schedule may vary by season.

Sightseeing Highlights

▲▲▲**The Cairns-Kuranda Railway** was an engineering marvel of the late 1800s. Between 1886 and 1891, a team of more than 1,500 laborers carved this 34-km (21-mile) narrow-gauge track from the side of a mountain using picks, shovels, and dynamite. They installed 15 tunnels, 98 curves, and dozens of bridges in the 1,055-foot climb from lush canefields up the Barron River Gorge to Kuranda village on the edge of the Atherton Tableland.

Today, tourists can make the same dramatic journey in colonial-style railcars for a round-trip price of around

A$35. After leaving Cairns (or the alternate restaurant-depot in suburban Freshwater), the train climbs past Horseshoe Bend, with vast views across the checkerboard of canefields to the Coral Sea. (On clear days, you can easily pick out Green Island on the Great Barrier Reef.) After passing Stony Creek Falls, there are breathtaking views of the precipitous Barron River Gorge wherever breaks in the dense rain forest vegetation allow. The train finally emerges at the great Barron Falls, a short distance from Kuranda.

▲**Barron Falls** must have been magnificent before its powerful waters were harnessed by a major hydroelectric project. A small quantity of water is still allowed to trickle over the huge rock wall—more, of course, during rainy season—to allow visitors to imagine the former grandeur of this great cataract. The train makes a photo stop at the Falls Lookout at the end of the Barron Falls Road from Kuranda. There's also a track from the lookout to the bottom of the gorge for hiking diehards.

▲**Kuranda Railway Station** is a lovely relic of bygone days. Built in 1915, it is an oasis in the midst of a tropical jungle and is itself a greenhouse of hanging ferns.

▲**Kuranda** (pop. 500) lives up to its billing as "the village in the rain forest." Its tree-lined main street, which leads about a half mile from the station to the market, features numerous arts and crafts galleries and Devonshire tea shops. Horse-drawn carts travel the short route.

Wednesday, Friday, and Sunday are market days in Kuranda. The open-air **Kuranda Market**, winding around a hill and across a small stream at the west end of town, gives local artisans and fruit growers a chance to sell their wares and produce. Here's where you'll find hand-painted T-shirts, leather goods, pottery, and woodwork, as well as tropical delights like mangoes, starfruit, and custard apples. The market is open rain or shine, April to October, Wednesdays and Fridays 9:00 a.m. to 12:00 noon, Sundays 9:00 a.m. to 1:00 p.m.

▲▲**Tjapukai Dance Theatre**, Australia's only Aboriginal

professional troupe, has performed all over the world. One-hour stage shows combine traditional and modern cultural themes, including Dreamtime legends, songs, and skills. Dancers draw rounds of laughter as they describe their body ornaments and tribal artifacts, to the haunting drone of ancient dijeridu music. Shows begin at 11:00 a.m. and 1:30 p.m. daily. Tickets are A$13 (children half-price).

▲▲**Australian Butterfly Sanctuary**, just outside town, is the largest of its type in the world. Approximately 2,000 butterflies of at least 35 species flit past your nose as you wander through tropical forest and around fern-fringed pools. Among them are the Cairns birdwing, a giant fluorescent green species; the Ulysses, electric blue and black; and the rare red lacewing. Open 10:00 a.m. to 3:00 p.m. daily; admission is A$8.50.

▲**Kuranda Wildlife Noctarium**, across the road from the market, is an indoor zoo with simulated forest conditions for nocturnal Australian fauna such as wombats, echnidnas, and opossums. It's open 10:00 a.m. to 4:00 p.m. daily; admission is A$7.

Also in Kuranda you'll find the **Honey House**, where bees in glass hives produce honey sold behind the counter (free admission); the **Cape York Experience**, an audiovisual program screening daily at Kuranda Village Centre (admission A$5); and the **Jilli Binna Museum**, a display of Aboriginal rain forest artifacts (admission A$1).

CAIRNS TO BRISBANE

Take a midmorning flight south to Brisbane, check into your hotel, then join the "koala cruise" to Lone Pine Koala Sanctuary, Brisbane's No. 1 tourist sight. If you ever wanted a photo of yourself holding one of these seemingly cuddly creatures, here's where to have it taken. The cruise winds its way up the meandering Brisbane River. After a dinner of mud crab or Moreton Bay bug, check out the evening offerings at the Queensland Cultural Centre.

Suggested Schedule

4:45 a.m.	Rise early and take a shuttle bus to the Cairns airport.
6:00 a.m.	Australian Flight 6 to Brisbane.
8:00 a.m.	Arrive at Brisbane. Take a shuttle bus 10 km to downtown hotel.
9:30 a.m.	Walking tour of downtown, followed by lunch.
1:00 p.m.	Board the "Koala Cruise" to Lone Pine Sanctuary.
4:30 p.m.	Return to downtown Brisbane by coach.
5:00 p.m.	Relax for a while in your hotel room.
6:00 p.m.	Dinner.
7:30 p.m.	Dive into culture at the Performing Arts Complex. Or sleep to recover from your early morning.

Brisbane Orientation

It has only been in recent years that Brisbane has outgrown its reputation as a "big country town" and developed a bit of sophistication. Now that it has tasted the cultured life, though, it shows no signs of backing off.

Queensland's capital, a city of 1.3 million people, sprawls for an amazing 471 square miles around both banks of the Brisbane River. (That makes it the third-largest city in the world in area.) Its downtown core, however, is relatively small, swallowing up a single horseshoe bend some 30 km upriver from Moreton Bay.

Like several other Australian cities, Brisbane (pronounced "Briz-b'n") got its start as a convict settlement. British Lieutenant John Oxley founded the colony in 1824. Agricultural and mining wealth from the vast inland reaches of the state made the city prosperous in the late nineteenth and early twentieth centuries. Today, Brisbane has blossomed into a progressive garden city.

Most of the main streets in downtown Brisbane have been named after British rulers, so if you know your English history, this should come easy. From the direction of the airport, in northeast Brisbane, Ann Street is the principal thoroughfare leading into downtown. It skirts the central railway station and King George Square, essentially marking the northwestern edge of the city center. Albert Street, running at right angles to Ann Street through the square, is the main northwest-southeast artery. Ann is paralleled to the southeast by Adelaide, Queen, Elizabeth, Charlotte, Mary, Margaret, and Alice streets, with the Botanic Gardens taking the southernmost chunk of the "horseshoe." Albert is paralleled to the southwest by George and William streets, and to the northeast by Edward, Creek, and Wharf streets. King George Square, on which sites the City Hall, and Queen Street between Albert and Edward are pedestrian malls.

The symbol of Brisbane's newfound refinement is the Queensland Cultural Centre, a fine and performing arts complex on the banks of the river, across from downtown. Beside the complex, covering 99 acres and spreading for a full kilometer down the Brisbane River, is the former site of World Expo '88, the single largest event in Australian history. A five-year, A$1 billion redevelopment of this world's fair site is scheduled for completion in 1994. Park areas, entertainment facilities, and indoor and outdoor eating spots are projected.

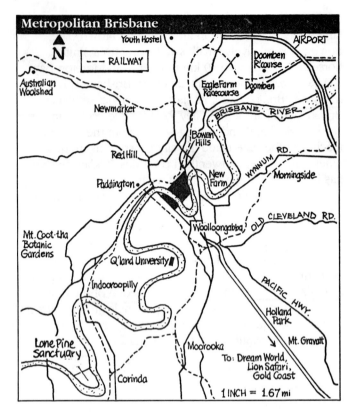

Brisbane has a subtropical climate, with warm, rainy summers (temperatures range from 67 to 85° F) and drier winters (49 to 69° F).

A Sightseeing Highlight
▲▲▲**Lone Pine Koala Sanctuary**, on the banks of the Brisbane River off Jesmond Road in Fig Tree Pocket, 11 km (7 mi.) from the city center, has more koalas (over 100) than any other wildlife reserve in Australia. You can have your photo taken cuddling one of the creatures (beware the sharp claws), visit the maternity wing and see newborn koalas, and feed the freely roaming kangaroos and emus. There are a variety of other Australian

animals, birds, and reptiles in the park as well. Open daily 9:15 a.m. to 4:45 p.m. Adult admission is A$9.

You can reach the Lone Pine Sanctuary on your own by taking a No. 84 bus from Adelaide Street. Better yet, if you've got an afternoon free, as we do, join the Koala Cruise (tel. 229-7055) leaving daily at 1:00 p.m. from Queens Wharf Road, North Quay (near downtown). The cruise costs A$24; combined with a return coach tour, it's A$32.

City Transportation

Coachtrans (tel. 236-1730) provides shuttle bus service to downtown Brisbane from the domestic and international airport terminals, a distance of some 13 km (8 mi.). Buses run half-hourly, and the charge is A$6. (You can also catch a No. 160 city bus for A$1.80.) Taxis charge about A$17 over the same distance. Several car rental agencies have desks at the airport, but you probably won't need a car for the remainder of your stay.

Within the city, Queensland Railways' electric Citytrain (tel. 225-0211) and City Council buses (tel. 225-4444) provide service to nearly all points. Six Citytrain lines extend some 45 km (28 mi.) east-west from Shorncliffe to Ipswich, 75 km (45 mi.) north-south from Caboolture to Beenleigh. Trains operate daily from approximately 4:30 a.m. to 1:30 a.m. (with limited hours on weekends). A one-segment fare is A$1. Bus tickets are A90 cents for one zone, A$1.30 for two, A$1.80 for three, or you can buy a A$5 Day Rover ticket providing unlimited bus transport for one day (5:30 a.m. to 11:30 p.m.). There's also a Brisbane River Ferry Service (tel. 399-4768) providing river crossings at several points for just A50 cents. Brisbane Bicycle Sales, 50 Albert Street (tel. 229-2433), has bicycles for rent at A$6 an hour or A$15 an 8-hour day.

For tourists, the **City Sights** bus runs an hourly circuit to 20 points of interest around Brisbane. All-day tickets are A$9.

Where to Stay

Brisbane is among the more expensive Australian cities for overnight stays, and it's not getting any cheaper. Its two newest major hotels—the **Hilton International**, 190 Elizabeth Street (tel. 07/321-3131), and the **Sheraton Brisbane**, 249 Turbot Street (tel. 835-3535)—are luxury, world-class accommodations. The Hilton features a 25-story garden atrium, while the 441-room Sheraton looms directly above the central station.

A step down in price is the **Mayfair Crest International**, a business person's favorite at Ann and Roma streets, King George Square (tel. 229-9111). The **Brisbane City Travelodge**, Roma Street near George Street (tel. 238-2222), is one of Brisbane's best bargains, with luxury-class facilities at moderate prices.

The **Yale Inner-City Inn**, 413 Upper Edward Street (tel. 832-1663), is a bed-and-breakfast guest house extremely popular among economy travelers. **Marrs Town House**, 391 Wickham Terrace (tel. 831-5388), is a newer accommodation near Albert Park, while the **Astor Motel**, 193 Wickham Terrace (tel. 831-9522), is another standby.

It used to be that youth hostelers had to travel 8 km north of downtown to find a bunk. Now, there's a new **Brisbane City YHA** at 56 Quay Street (tel. 236-1004). Also in town are a pair of independent **Brisbane Backpackers Inns**—at 71 Kent Street, New Farm (tel. 385-4504), and at 175 Given Terrace (tel. 368-1047).

Where to Eat

No one is accusing Brisbane of being the gastronomic capital of Australia. But there are a number of good restaurants, as befits a city of this size.

The southeast Queensland coast is renowned for its seafood—particularly the Moreton Bay bugs (a lobster relation) and the Queensland mud crabs. You can't go wrong ordering them at **Gambaro's**, a casual café just west of downtown at 34 Caxton Street, Petrie Terrace; or

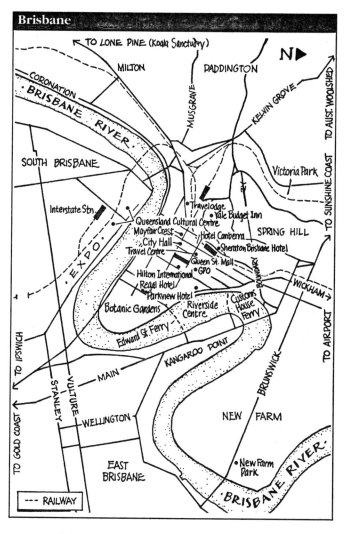

Brisbane

TO LONE PINE (Koala Sanctuary)

N ▶

MILTON   PADDINGTON

CORONATION

BRISBANE RIVER

MUSGRAVE

KELVIN GROVE

TO AUST. WOOLSHED

SOUTH BRISBANE

Victoria Park

TO SUNSHINE COAST

Interstate Stn.

Travelodge

Yale Budget Inn

Queensland Cultural Centre

Mayfair Crest

Hotel Camberra

SPRING HILL

City Hall

Sheraton Brisbane Hotel

Travel Centre

Queen St. Mall

GPO

Hilton International

Regal Hotel

Parkview Hotel

EXPO

BOUNDARY

WICKHAM →

TO AIRPORT

Botanic Gardens

Riverside Centre

Customs House Ferry

Edward St. Ferry

KANGAROO POINT

BRUNSWICK

TO IPSWICH

MAIN

VULTURE

STANLEY

WELLINGTON

NEW   FARM

TO GOLD COAST ←

EAST BRISBANE

New Farm Park

BRISBANE RIVER

--- RAILWAY

the **Breakfast Creek Wharf**, east of the central city at 190 Breakfast Creek Road, Newstead.

In the central city area, the best upmarket dining is in the best hotels. **Michael's Riverside**, in the new Riverside Centre at 123 Eagle Street, wins plaudits for its high-brow French cuisine. But many casual, less expensive spots are fun, too—like **Jimmy's on the Mall**, a licensed, open-air restaurant in the Queen Street Mall. In the Elizabeth Arcade off Charlotte Street, **Tortilla** (Aussies pronounce the "L"s) is an atmospheric choice for decent Mexican food and **The Source** has good, cheap vegetarian offerings. **Mama Luigi's**, 240 St. Paul's Terrace, is a longtime Italian favorite, and you can eat like a Russian at **Czars**, 47 Elizabeth Street.

The adjacent suburbs of Fortitude Valley and New Farm, walking distance east of downtown (via Ann or Wickham streets), feature many authentic, low-priced ethnic restaurants. Try **Giardinetto's** (Italian), 336 Brunswick Street; **Cathay** (Chinese), 222 Wickham Street; and **Baan Thai** (Thai), 630 Brunswick Street. Farther toward the airport, the **Breakfast Creek Hotel**, 2 Kingsford Smith Drive, has a nationally famous steak-and-beer garden.

In Petrie Terrace, **Michel Bonet**, 2 Caxton Street, has a reputation as Brisbane's best French restaurant. The **Caxton Garden Grill**, in the Caxton Hotel, provides jazz accompaniment to meals. In nearby Paddington, the **Makassan**, 215 Given Terrace, offers a rare Asian delight: Indonesian cuisine.

Nightlife
The **Performing Arts Complex**, in the Queensland Cultural Centre, contains the Concert Hall for symphonic performances, the Lyric Theatre for opera, ballet, drama, and musical comedy, and the Cremorne Theatre for smaller and experimental productions. Almost any major performance will be presented here. Event schedules can be obtained and bookings made by calling 844-0201 or visiting the PAC box office. The Cultural Centre is on the south side of the Brisbane River at Grey and Melbourne streets.

Other good spots for live theater include the **S.G.I.O. Theatre**, Turbot and Albert streets, home of the Queensland Theatre Company; and **La Boite**, 57 Hale

Street in Milton, home of the Brisbane Repertory Company. Queensland film censors are more protective of viewers than in other states, but you'll find a good number of movie theaters in the downtown area, especially on Albert Street.

Brisbane's most popular disco-nightclub, at this writing, was the **Brisbane Underground**, Caxton and Hal streets in Paddington, open until 3:00 a.m. Wednesday through Saturday. The major hotels all have their posh night spots.

For live music, try **The Roxy**, Brunswick and St. Paul streets in Fortitude Valley, for rock; the **Brisbane Jazz Club**, Kangaroo Point, for jazz; or the **Treasury Hotel**, Elizabeth and George streets, for blues. **Wilson's 1870**, 103 Queen Street, appeals to an older crowd, with a piano bar and cocktail music.

Helpful Hints

The **Brisbane Visitors and Convention Bureau** (tel. 221-8411), in City Hall on the west side of King George Square, is open weekdays 8:30 a.m. to 5:00 p.m. The **Queensland Government Travel Centre** is at 196 Adelaide Street (tel. 221-6111), open 9:00 a.m. to 4:45 p.m. Monday through Friday, 9:00 to 11:15 a.m. Saturday. There are tourist information booths in the Queen Street Mall and the Brisbane Transit Centre on Roma Street. The **Central Post Office** on Queen Street is open Monday through Friday, 7:00 a.m. to 7:00 p.m. **Banking** hours are 9:30 a.m. to 4:00 p.m. Monday through Thursday, to 5:00 p.m. Friday. Retail shops in the central city are open 8:15 a.m. to 5:00 p.m. Monday through Thursday, to 9:00 p.m. Friday, to 12:00 noon Saturday. It's hard to find anything open on a Sunday.

There's an **American Consulate** at 383 Wickham Terrace (tel. 839-8955). In case of emergencies, dial 000. There's also a 24-hour number for medical service: 378-6900.

BRISBANE AND THE GOLD COAST

Take a bus to the Gold Coast, Australia's version of
Miami Beach. Depending on how much Brisbane sightseeing you want to squeeze in before you go, you can
have the entire afternoon on the beach—for that tan
you'll want to show off when you get home.

Suggested Schedule	
8:00 a.m.	Breakfast at hotel.
9:00 a.m.	If you like, visit one or two Brisbane attractions or join a half-day city tour.
Open	Board a bus for the Gold Coast. It's a 1-hour trip to Surfers Paradise. Upon arrival, check into your hotel and hit the beach.
6:00 p.m.	Relax at hotel.
7:00 p.m.	Dinner.
9:00 p.m.	As they say in Australia, "Rage!" In North America, we'd say, "Party on!"

Brisbane Sightseeing Highlights
▲▲▲**The Queensland Cultural Centre** occupies a
14.7-acre site on the south bank of the Brisbane River,
facing the city center across the Victoria Bridge. A series
of distinctive white structures set amid landscaped gardens, sculptures, and water malls, this A$173 million
complex has four components: the Queensland Art
Gallery (opened in 1982), the Performing Arts Complex
(1985), the Queensland Museum (1986), and the State
Library (1988). A convention center, three restaurants,
four cafeterias, and several specialty shops are among
its facilities. The Queensland Cultural Centre Trust (tel.
240-7229) has full information.

    The Queensland Art Gallery (tel. 240-7333) dis-
plays its permanent collection of Australian and
European art, plus numerous touring shows, in 15 sepa-

rate exhibition areas. A wide variety of lectures, work-shops, and musical performances are regularly offered. There's free admission to the gallery, open daily 10:00 a.m. to 5:00 p.m., Wednesday to 8:00 p.m. Guided tours are available weekdays at 11:00 a.m., 1:00 and 2:00 p.m., and weekends at 2:00 and 3:00 p.m., for no additional charge.

The 124-year-old **Queensland Museum** (tel. 240-7633), relocated from a nineteenth-century building, has three floors of displays emphasizing the state's geology and natural history, Aboriginal roots and Melanesian influences, pioneer history, and early technology. Popular with children is a large outdoor Dinosaur Garden. Open daily 9:00 a.m. to 5:00 p.m., Wednesday to 8:00 p.m. Admission is free.

The **Performing Arts Complex** (tel. 240-7483) attracted nearly 1 million patrons to its three theaters during its first two years of operation (see Nightlife, Day 19). Performers included the Royal Shakespeare Company, the Bolshoi Ballet, and the London Philharmonic Orchestra. Guided tours are offered hourly, 10:00 a.m. to 4:00 p.m., Monday through Saturday, for A$9.50. There are backstage tours on selected days by reservation for A$10.

▲**Mount Coot-tha Botanic Gardens**, Toowong, features native and imported plants in tropical rain forest, subtropical, and desert settings. They're open daily 7:00 a.m. to 5:00 p.m. The Sir Thomas Brisbane Planetarium offers a stargazing show from Wednesday through Sunday between 12:00 noon and 7:00 p.m.; bookings are essential (A$7). Atop Mount Coot-tha, 8 km (5 miles) from the city center, is a restaurant with panoramic views all the way to Moreton Bay. Other major gardens in Brisbane include the City Botanic Gardens at the south end of Albert Street; New Farm Park, east of downtown off Brunswick Street; and Newstead Park on Breakfast Creek Road, harboring Brisbane's oldest building, the 1846 Newstead House.

▲▲**The Australian Woolshed**, 15 km (9 miles) north-west of downtown at 148 Samford Road, Ferny Hills, is as close as you're likely to get to an authentic Aussie sheep station in a metropolitan area. Working sheepdogs demonstrate their skill, and there are exhibits of wool classing and spinning. Admission of A$8 includes a shearing demonstration and parade of trained rams at 10:45 a.m. daily and 2:00 p.m. Sunday. The craft shop has been voted Australia's best. The complex normally is open daily 9:30 a.m. to 5:00 p.m., although its licensed outback-style restaurant features "bush dances" (A$26) on Friday and Saturday from 7:00 p.m. to 12:00 midnight.

▲**Earlystreet Historical Village**, 75 McIlwraith Avenue, Norman Park, is a collection of eight historic Queensland buildings set in five acres of colonial gardens surrounding the nineteenth-century Eulalia Manor. You'll find an old slab hut, a shearers' pub, a general store, a black-smith's shop, a coach house, and several residences, all relocated to this site and refurnished in mid-1800s style. Classified by the National Trust, the village is open weekdays 9:30 a.m. to 4:30 p.m., Saturday and Sunday from 10:30 a.m. Admission is A$9.

▲**The Kookaburra Queen** is an elegant wooden paddle wheeler that cruises the waters of the Brisbane River several times daily. Ninety-minute tea or snack cruises, leaving at 10:00 a.m. (daily except Saturday), 12:45 p.m. (weekdays), and 3:00 p.m. (Sundays), cost A$25. Daily dinner cruises, boarding at 7:00 p.m., are priced from A$45 to A$55. The Queen leaves from the Petrie Bight Marina on Howard Street, at the east end of the city near the National Hotel. **Paddington Circle** is the quaintest shopping area in Brisbane. Merchants have retained and restored the suburb's original colonial architecture to give the entire district a heritage feeling. Most of the shops are along Given Terrace and Latrobe Terrace.

▲**City tours** are something I'm not normally crazy about —mainly because I prefer to explore a new place on my own time—but given the limited time allotted to Brisbane

in this itinerary, a bus tour may be the most efficient way
to see the main attractions. Half-day tours of 3 to 3½
hours, beginning about 9:00 a.m., cost A$22 at this writ-
ing; check with Ansett Pioneer (tel. 226-1184),
Boomerang Tours (tel. 236-3614), or Magic Carpet Tours
(tel. 345-8300). Better yet, take advantage of the **City
Sights** bus circuit for A$9 (see City Transportation, Day
19).

Getting to the Gold Coast
Except in the middle of the night, you'll never have to
wait longer than an hour or two to catch a bus from
Brisbane to Australia's favorite beach resort area.
Greyhound and Coachtrans buses leave at least ten times
a day from the Roma Street Transit Centre. Coachtrans
buses offer direct shuttle service from the Gold Coast to
Brisbane International Airport. The fare is A$11.50.
Remember to allow 1½ hours for the trip from Surfers,
2 hours from Coolangatta.

There's talk of opening a rail link between Brisbane
and the Gold Coast, but it hasn't happened yet.

Gold Coast Orientation
A glittering white sand beach stretching 32 km (20 mi.)
down the coast of southeasternmost Queensland, just 65
km (40 mi.) from Brisbane, the Gold Coast is the single
most popular resort strip in Australia. That has both good
and bad connotations. There are hotels, restaurants, and
night spots of all standards and prices, a lush mountain
backdrop not far from the lovely beach, and an incredible variety of manmade attractions. But there's also a
great deal of crass commercialism and tourist kitsch prey-
ing on the throngs in transition. Overlook that and you'll
have a great time.

At least a dozen separate communities, linked by the
busy Gold Coast Highway, comprise the city of Gold
Coast. About 265,000 people make their home along this
narrow strip, five times the population of a quarter-century

ago. Southport, the Gold Coast's northernmost community, is its commercial and industrial center. Surfers
Paradise, the next main center reached heading south, is
the Waikiki-style high-rise capital of the coast and the
site of its most frenetic nightlife. Halfway down the coast
is Burleigh Heads, a laid-back, family community at the
foot of fauna-rich Burleigh Heads National Park.
Coolangatta marks not only the southern extreme of the
Gold Coast but also the boundary between Queensland
and New South Wales. The Gold Coast Airport, with
direct links to Sydney, Melbourne, Adelaide, and other
cities, is here.

Local Transportation
Don't worry about being stuck on the Gold Coast without
a car. You can either base yourself in one town and cope
quite nicely or you can call upon Surfside buses (tel. 36-
7666) for regular transportation links between Southport
and Coolangatta. A Day Rover ticket is A$6.35. Silly Sycle,
6 Beach Road, Surfers, will rent you a bike or moped.

Where to Stay
As Surfers Paradise (usually called "Surfers") is the center
of most of the action, we'll deal with it first. At the top of
the line is the elegant **Gold Coast International Hotel**,
Gold Coast Highway and Staghorn Avenue (tel. 075/92-
1200); just a notch back is the **Ramada at Paradise
Center**, Gold Coast Highway and Hanlan Street (tel.
075/59-3400). The **Chevron Paradise Hotel**, 15 Ferny
Avenue (tel. 39-0444), is a good choice in the high moderate range; check out the **Sands Courtesy Inn**, 40 The
Esplanade (tel. 39-8433), in the low moderate area.
You're reaching a bit to find a good economy room in
Surfers, but the **Delilah Motel**, Ferny and Cypress
avenues (tel. 38-1722), will do quite nicely. The best budget accommodation in Surfers is the **Backpackers Motor
Inn**, 2835 Gold Coast Highway (tel. 38-7250), nearly a
mile south of the town center.

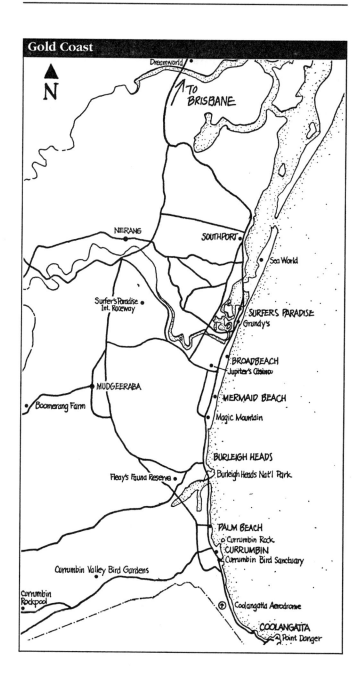

Gold Coast

N

Dreamworld
TO BRISBANE

NERANG

SOUTHPORT

Sea World

Surfer's Paradise
Int. Raceway

SURFERS PARADISE
Grundy's

BROADBEACH
Jupiter's Casino

MUDGEERABA

MERMAID BEACH

Boomerang Farm

Magic Mountain

BURLEIGH HEADS

Fleay's Fauna Reserve

Burleigh Heads Nat'l Park

PALM BEACH

Currumbin Rock

CURRUMBIN
Currumbin Bird Sanctuary

Currumbin Valley Bird Gardens

Currumbin
Rockpool

Coolangatta Aerodrome

COOLANGATTA
Point Danger

The Gold Coast's best accommodations—all of them world class—are the **Conrad International Hotel and Jupiter's Casino**, Gold Coast Highway, Broadbeach Island (tel. 075/92-1133); the **Hyatt Regency Sanctuary Cove**, Hope Island (tel. 30-1234); and the **Sheraton Mirage Gold Coast**, Sea World Drive (tel. 91-1488). You'll find moderate- and economy-priced motels all along the Gold Coast Highway from here south, but Coolangatta is the king in these price ranges. Try the **Pacific Village Motel**, 88 Marine Parade (tel. 36-2733), or the **Bombora Holiday Lodge**, Marine Parade at Dutton Street (tel. 36-1888). The **Backpackers Inn**, 45 McLean Street, Coolangatta (tel. 36-2422), costs A$12 a night and has a licensed restaurant and bar on the premises.

Where to Eat

There are as many different kinds of places to eat on the Gold Coast as there are kinds of people who visit, and that's a lot. The coast's characterization as a utopia for junk-food junkies is not totally inaccurate, but there is no shortage of more wholesome dining establishments.

In Surfers, try the **Rusty Pelican**, Orchid and Elkhorn avenues, or the **Captain's Tale**, 5 Cavill Avenue on the mall, for seafood; **Pellegrini**, 3120 Gold Coast Highway, for Italian cuisine; or **Shogun**, 90 Bundall Road, for Japanese food. Be warned, however: none of them are cheap. You can spend less money and have a lot of fun at the hofbrau-style **Bavarian Steak House**, Gold Coast Highway at Cavill Avenue; the **Tandoori Taj** (North Indian), 3100 Gold Coast Highway; the **Mexican Kitchen**, 150 Bundall Road; or the **Athens** (Greek), Gold Coast Highway near Laycock Street. The **Surfer's Deli**, 25 Orchid Avenue, is a pleasant sidewalk café with light meals and entertainment.

Up and down the coast, the **Holy Mackerel**, 174 Marine Parade, Labrador (north of Southport), offers free shuttle service from Surfers to its seafood restaurant.

Mermaid Beach has a good Italian restaurant, **Gino's Osteria**, 2563 Gold Coast Highway, and nearby on the same road, the most passionately named vegetarian eatery I've ever heard of—the **Lusty Lentil**.

Farther down, in Burleigh Heads, the **Chieng Mai Thai** restaurant is at 31 James Street. Finally, no south-end budget watcher should pass up a A$5 counter meal at the **Queensland Hotel**, Boundary Street, Coolangatta.

Nightlife

The cards are dealt 24 hours a day at **Jupiter's Casino** in the Conrad International Hotel on Broadbeach Island. Blackjack, roulette, craps, baccarat, keno, and several other games are played continuously in this sophisticated new casino. There are also several restaurants and a showroom featuring world-class entertainers.

In Surfers, the overloaded disco-cabaret lineup includes such standouts as **Twains International** and the five-story **Penthouse**, both on Orchid Avenue. The **Swingin' Vine**, 47A Cavill Avenue, is noted for jazz and comedy. Ask for directions to **Bombay Rock**, the best of several clubs in Surfers that feature live rock. Its counterpart, 13 km (8 miles) south of Surfers in North Palm Beach, is the **Playroom**, on the Gold Coast Highway opposite the Tallebudgera Bridge.

There's cheaper entertainment just across the New South Wales border from Coolangatta in the town of Tweed Heads. The club scene flourishes here where poker machines ("one-armed bandits") are legal. Meals, drinks, and top-flight entertainment are always reduced in price to entice you to play the pokies. They're technically membership clubs, but out-of-state visitors, especially foreigners, are welcome. Shuttle buses can run you from Surfers or elsewhere on the Gold Coast to such spots as **Twin Towns Services Club**, Wharf Street; **Tweed Heads Bowls Club**, Tweed Street; and my favorite, **Seagulls Rugby League Football Club**, Gollan Drive.

For romancers or real budget-watchers, there's nothing cheaper than a walk on a moonlit beach.

Helpful Hints
The **Gold Coast Visitors and Convention Bureau** has its main offices in the Cavill Mall, Surfers Paradise (tel. 38-4419). (There's a Coolangatta branch: tel. 26-7765.) You'll also find the Queensland Government Travel Centre here on the second floor of the TAA Building, 38-40 Cavill Avenue (tel. 92-1033). All are open 9:00 a.m. to 4:45 p.m. weekdays, 9:00 to 11:15 a.m. Saturday.

The Surfers Paradise **post office** is at the corner of Cavill Avenue and the Gold Coast Highway. **Banking** hours are 9:30 a.m. to 4:00 p.m. Monday through Thursday, to 5:00 p.m. Friday. Retail shops are open daily except Sunday, 9:00 a.m to 5:30 p.m.

In case of emergencies, dial 000. For 24-hour medical assistance, call 38-8823.

THE GOLD COAST

Your final day on Australian beaches. Why not decide for yourself if the name "Surfers Paradise" really fits? Or dive into a grab bag of tourist attractions such as Sea World, the Currumbin Bird Sanctuary, or the Mudgeeraba Boomerang Farm.

Suggested Schedule

7:30 a.m.	Up and at 'em, unless you need extra sleep to recover from last night's fling.
9:00 a.m.	Visit the Currumbin Bird Sanctuary near Palm Beach.
11:00 a.m.	Catch a few late morning rays.
12:30 p.m.	Lunch.
1:30 p.m.	Sea World is worth a full afternoon.
5:00 p.m.	Head back to your hotel. Take a quick dip in the pool.
6:30 p.m.	Dinner.
8:00 p.m.	It's your last night in Australia—what you do with it is up to you.

Sightseeing Highlights

▲▲**The Currumbin Bird Sanctuary**, just off the Gold Coast Highway on Tomewin Street, Currumbin, 18 km (11 miles) south of Surfers, is a tourist favorite mainly because of the flocks of brightly colored rainbow lorikeets that fly in daily from their homes in the wild to be fed from plates of honey held by willing visitors. Arrive before 10:00 a.m. to see the mass of orange-breasted, blue-headed, green-backed birds, or wait until about 4:00 in the afternoon. A variety of other native birds, koalas, kangaroos, and wallabies make their homes in the 50-acre wildlife refuge. You can walk among the critters or watch from a 2-km miniature railway. Numerous craftspersons ply their trades; among them are potters, glassblowers, and gem cutters. Open daily 8:00 a.m. to 5:00 p.m. Adult admission is A$12.

▲▲**Sea World**, on the spit 5 km (3 mi.) north of Surfers, is Australia's No. 1 marine theme park. Dolphins, killer whales, and sea lions alternately awe and amuse audiences in separate shows, as do acrobatic water skiers. The World of the Sea Theatre combines audiovisuals with live demonstrations of underwater diving and shark feeding. Visitors can pet dolphins, feed sea lions, and gaze at an enormous aquarium. The park's dozen rides include Australia's first free-fall waterslide (with a frightening five-story drop!) and its only triple-loop roller coaster, as well as a monorail and carousel for those with less intestinal fortitude.

Sea World is open daily (except Christmas) from 10:00 a.m. to 5:00 p.m. The adult admission of A$29 includes all rides and performances. Call 32-1055 or 32-5131 (recorded) for daily show times and bus connections.

▲**Dreamworld**, in Coomera 15 minutes toward Brisbane from Surfers, is Australia's largest Disney-style theme park. This 208-acre complex has a little of everything, some of which will remind you very much of parks in Anaheim and Orlando. You can see the Koala Country Music Show, for example, with 22 life-size but computerized Aussie animals doing the singing and playing. You can take any of 17 different rides, among them a steam train, a "Murrissippi River" cruise, and a high-speed trip through Avalanche Mountain. Sound familiar? Seventeen shops and eleven restaurants take care of shopping and hunger pangs.

Dreamworld is open Saturday through Wednesday 10:00 a.m. to 5:00 p.m., daily during school holiday periods. Adult admission of A$27 includes all rides and performances. Round-trip express bus service from the Gold Coast is offered for A$8.50 by Keith's Tours (tel. 30-5908).

Movieworld, off the Pacific Highway 20 km (12 miles) northwest of Surfers in Oxenford, provides Australia with a Universal Studios-type attraction. Created by Warner Brothers, this theme park re-creates movie sets and gives visitors looks at special effects and other inside knowledge of the film industry. Open 10:00 a.m. to 5:00 p.m. daily; adult admission is A$29.

Burleigh Heads National Park is a small, unexpected natural bushland oasis in the middle of this utterly commercial strip. Koalas, wallabies, bandicoots, and much birdlife inhabit this bluff overlooking the mouth of Tallebudgera Creek. A graded 3-km (2-mi.) walking track leads around the headland.

Mudgeeraba Boomerang Farm, on Springbrook Road 20 minutes inland from the Gold Coast, is not a major tourist attraction. Unlike others, however, it's uniquely Australian. Not only will the Hawes family sell you a boomerang made in their own factory but they'll also teach you how to throw it so that it comes back to you. Their 200-acre farm also has a fascinating boomerang museum. Open seven days a week. Ask directions locally or phone 30-5231.

▲Lamington National Park comprises some 50,000 acres of lushly forested mountains 43 km (27 mi.) from the Gold Coast via Nerang. Some call it "the Green behind the Gold." The park contains 140 km (87 mi.) of walking tracks, an estimated 500 waterfalls, and a forest of 3,000-year-old beech trees. Two small guest houses, at Binna Burra and O'Reilly's, serve park visitors.

Grundy's at Paradise Centre is the sort of place that shoppers and fun-seekers don't need to be told about: they'll find it on their own. Set dead center in Surfers Paradise, with direct access from the beach, Ramada Hotel, or Cavill Mall, this three-story complex includes 110 boutiques and specialty shops, an international food village and the most cacophonous collection of video games you've ever heard (or seen).

Pacific Fair, near the casino-hotel in Broadbeach, is the Gold Coast's other most interesting shopping center. The architects have re-created streets from all over the world—from Oxford Street (London) to the Boulevard St.-Michel (Paris), Basin Street (New Orleans) to Lindenstrasse (Berlin). Appropriate specialty shops intermingle with chain department stores.

FLY HOME FROM BRISBANE

It's been a great 22 days. Board your flight home to the States this afternoon in Brisbane. Thanks to the International Date Line, you'll reach the U.S. West Coast only 1½ hours after leaving Australia. The longest day of your life was custom-made for savoring those great Australian memories.

Suggested Schedule

8:00 a.m.	Rise and shine, eat breakfast, and pack everything but your swim suit.
9:00 a.m.	You've got most of the day reserved for the beach.
4:00 p.m.	Grab a Vegemite sandwich for a snack, scoop up your bags, and board a bus for Brisbane airport.
5:30 p.m.	Arrive at the airport for check-in.
7:00 p.m.	Qantas Flight 117 leaves for Honolulu, with connections there to San Francisco, Los Angeles, and other cities in the U.S. and Canada.

Farewell Advice

Call your airline first thing in the morning to reconfirm your departure time. Hopefully, you will also have telephoned a couple days earlier from Brisbane to confirm your seat.

The buses of Skennars Transport (tel. 38-9444 in Surfers) offer direct shuttle service from the Gold Coast to Brisbane International Airport. The fare is A$11. Remember to allow 1½ hours for the trip from Surfers, 2 hours from Coolangatta.

When you reach Brisbane, instruct the driver that you need the international terminal. The domestic terminal, where you arrived, is a considerable drive away, around the runways. Don't spend all your money before reaching the airport. You'll have to hold A$20 out to pay the airport departure tax. As you head back home across the Pacific, you can think back on a great three-week vacation—and where you want to go on your next trip Down Under.

The biggest frustration in trying to cover an entire continent in 22 days is omitting so many worthwhile spots from the itinerary. If you've got the time, the following options can be spliced into your schedule as follows:

Tasmania—Leave from and return to Melbourne (Day 8).

Adelaide and/or Perth—Between Melbourne and Alice Springs (Day 11).

Darwin—Between Alice Springs and Cairns (Day 16).

Great Barrier Reef Islands—Between Cairns and Brisbane (Day 19).

TASMANIA

Australia's island state, some 230 km (143 miles) across Bass Strait from Victoria, is almost a world unto itself. Like a cross between New England and the Pacific Northwest, its colonial manors are scattered through the lowlands beneath forested mountain peaks.

Suggested 6-Day Schedule	
Day 1	Arrive in Devonport from Melbourne. Rent a car and drive to Launceston.
Day 2	See Cataract Gorge, then drive down the east coast via Bicheno to Port Arthur.
Day 3	After exploring the former penal colony in the morning, drive to Hobart via Richmond.
Day 4	Catch the view from Mount Wellington, then drive via Lake St. Clair and Queenstown to Strahan.
Day 5	Go on the Gordon River cruise in the morning, then drive to Stanley for the night.
Day 6	Putter down the north coast to Devonport. Night flight or ferry voyage back to Melbourne.

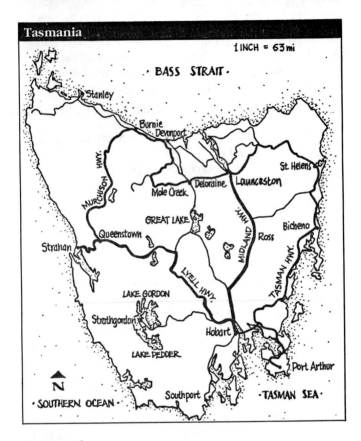

Getting There

As many as 14 flights daily transit the Bass Strait between Melbourne and Hobart (the state capital), Launceston, Devonport, and Burnie/Wynyard. The flight takes 65 minutes to Hobart, 55 minutes to Launceston, 50 minutes to the other two north coast towns. Round-trip air fares, at this writing, were in the A$150 range. There are also direct flights several times a week to Launceston and Hobart from Sydney and the Gold Coast.

An overnight ferry, the *Abel Tasman*, crosses the strait every other day at 6:00 p.m., arriving in Devonport at 8:30 the following morning. Return boats leave

Devonport at 6:00 p.m. the following day. One-way fares vary according to season and facilities but range from A$104 (winter) to A$144 (summer) on the low end to A$212 to A$295 at the high end.

A new high-speed passenger-only catamaran service operates between Port Welshpool, Victoria (south of Melbourne), and George Town, Tasmania (north of Launceston). The service operates daily mid-December through January, daily except Tuesday from February through April and October to mid-December, and daily except Tuesday and Thursday the rest of the year. Boats leave George Town at 8:30 a.m., arriving in Victoria at 1:00 p.m.; then depart Port Welshpool at 2:00 p.m., arriving back in Tasmania at 6:30 p.m. Adult one-way fares are A$114 to A$120.

Getting Around
The large auto rental firms—Hertz, Avis, Thrifty, and Budget—are represented in all large towns in Tasmania. Weekly rates, including unlimited kilometers are similar, ranging from A$270 to A$1,050 depending on class of vehicle.

If you're a solo budget traveler, look into the seven-day "Tassie Pass" with **Tasmanian Redline Coaches** for A$99. (A 14-day pass is only A$120.) Book through the Tasmanian Travel Centre (see "Helpful Hints"). The Redline terminal in Devonport is at 9 Edward Street (tel. 004/24-2585); in Launceston at 112 George Street (tel. 003/31-9177); in Hobart at 96 Harrington Street (tel. 004/34-4577).

Sightseeing Highlights
▲**Devonport** (pop. 25,000) is the market center of the fertile north coast region. **Tigarra**, atop the headland called Mersey Bluff, remembers the culture of the Tasmanian Aboriginal, one of the most tragic races in history. Early settlers hunted down and shot the native Tasmanians until a mere handful survived. They were

resettled off Tasmania's north coast, on Flinders Island, where the last one died in 1876. Also in Devonport are the **Don River Railway Museum**, the **Maritime Museum**, and **Taswegia** history printery and craft gallery.

▲**Launceston** is Tasmania's second city, both in population (65,000) and age (founded in 1805, a year after Hobart). Situated at the head of the tranquil Tamar River, it is noted for its many parks and gardens, especially **Cataract Gorge**. Reminiscent of the Wisconsin Dells, it is surrounded by a rhododendron garden and crossed by an aerial chair lift. Also see the **Queen Victoria Museum and Art Gallery** and the **Waverly Woollen Mills** (tours daily 9:00 a.m. to 4:00 p.m.). Thirteen km (8 miles) west of Launceston, near Hadspen, is the beautiful **Entally House** historic homestead, built in 1819.

▲▲▲**Port Arthur** was a name synonymous with harsh justice in Australia's convict past. Between 1830 and 1877, some 12,500 hardened criminals lived in this isolated location under the threat of the lash and long-term solitary isolation that drove many to madness. Today, the restored **Port Arthur National Historic Site** commemorates the nation's roots like nowhere else.

Elsewhere on the Tasman Peninsula, you can see spectacular coastal formations—arches, undersea caves, and blowholes—that helped make this prison colony so difficult to escape. **The Bush Mill** theme park, 5 km (3 mi.) north of the historic site, recalls the days of the early timber cutters. The **Tasmanian Devil Park** at Taranna, another 5 km north, is a good place to see these varmints.

▲▲**Richmond** is a detour off the road back to Hobart, just 26 km (16 mi.) northeast of the capital. The treasures of this charming 1820s town include Australia's first bridge and its oldest Catholic church. The Richmond Gaol has been faithfully restored. Many of the community's elegant sandstone buildings now house Devonshire tea shops, arts and crafts galleries, and historical museums.

▲▲▲**Hobart**, Tasmania's capital and largest city (pop. 185,000), was established in 1804 as the second European settlement in Australia. The inner-city suburb of **Battery Point** is the original seamen's quarter, where tiny cottages share the narrow winding streets with Georgian mansions and Victorian terrace houses—now, as often as not, occupied by restaurants, bed and breakfasts, art galleries, and antique shops. **The Van Diemen's Land Memorial Folk Museum** in the Narryna mansion at 103 Hampden Road has a superb period collection. The **Maritime Museum of Tasmania** in the Secheron House mansion off Colville Street is also interesting.

Elsewhere in Hobart, see the excellent **Tasmanian Museum and Art Gallery**, the **Royal Tasmanian Botanical Gardens**, and the scale-model **Tudor Court** at Sandy Bay. The **Wrest Point Casino**, 410 Sandy Bay Road (tel. 25-0112), was Australia's first major gambling casino, and is still as lively as ever. From the summit of 4,170-foot Mount Wellington, a 20-km (12½-mi.) drive from the city center, you can savor the spectacular layout of this beautiful harbor city at the mouth of the Derwent River.

▲▲**Strahan**, a tiny fishing and timber port, is best known as the starting point for cruises through Macquarie Harbour and up the Gordon River, a crystalline stream that winds through unexplored rain forest between the **Franklin-Lower Gordon Wild Rivers National Park** and **South West National Park**. These two parks, as well as **Cradle Mountain-Lake St. Clair National Park** off the Lyell Highway at Derwent Bridge, en route from Hobart to Strahan, have been designated "World Heritage Areas" for their spectacular, untouched wilderness. Mount Everest conqueror Sir Edmund Hillary has called this region "the greatest walking country in the world." Some believe its denizens may include the legendary Tasmanian wolf, a striped marsupial canine last confirmed alive in the 1930s.

▲**Stanley** has changed little since it was established in 1826 by sheep breeders. Its combination of history and maritime beauty is accented by **The Nut**, a striking 500-foot mesalike basalt outcropping that dominates coastal scenery for many miles around.

▲**The Northwest Coast** drive, 129 km (80 mi.) along the Bass Highway from Stanley to Devonport, provides a final day of Tasmanian wanderings. **Rocky Cape National Park** contains Aboriginal caves, fields of wild orchids, and the glistening white sand **Sisters Beach** with Birdland Native Gardens reserve. **Lapoinya** rhododendron gardens are nearby. At **Wynyard**, you'll find **Fossil Bluff**, where the oldest marsupial fossil in Australia was discovered. **Burnie** (pop. 21,000) has a major timber products industry and the **Pioneer Village Museum**, re-creating the town's turn-of-the-century commercial center. Proceed east to the town of **Penguin**, which takes its name from colonies of fairy penguins living along the shore; **Ulverstone**, gateway to the Leven Canyon; and finally to **Devonport** and the *Abel Tasman* ferry terminal.

Helpful Hints

The **Tasmanian Travel Centre** has its head office at 80 Elizabeth Street, Hobart (tel. 002/30-0250). You'll find other offices along the route in Devonport (18 Rooke Street; tel. 004/24-1526); Launceston (St. John and Paterson streets; tel. 003/37-3111); and Burnie (48 Cattley Street; tel. 004/31-8111). Most of these offices are open from 8:45 a.m. to 5:45 p.m. weekdays, 9:00 to 11:00 a.m. Saturdays.

In Melbourne, inquire at 256 Collins Street (tel. 03/653-7999) and in Sydney at 149 King Street (tel. 02/233-2500). In North America, write to Australia Naturally, Suite 1270, 2121 Avenue of the Stars, Los Angeles, CA 09967 (tel. 310/553-6352).

Two publications produced by the Tasmanian Travel Centre are invaluable. *The Visitor's Guide to Tasmania* will tell you about every tourist attraction in the state. The bimonthly *Tasmanian Travelways* newspaper tells you how to get there, where to stay and where to eat, and how much it will cost you.

ADELAIDE AND SOUTH AUSTRALIA

South Australia is known as the "Festival State" for its many annual events and as the "WOW" state for its wine, opals, and wildlife. The Barossa Valley northeast of Adelaide is Australia's premier wine-producing district; Coober Pedy, in the state's scorching outback, is the country's best-known opal mining center; and Kangaroo Island, off the south coast, may have a richer concentration of native fauna than any other part of the nation.

Adelaide, the pleasant capital of South Australia, is a perfect staging point for reaching these and other outlying attractions. Though Adelaide, with few points of major tourist interest, may come across to visitors as "a big country town," its urban population of 1.05 million is nearly three-quarters of the entire state. The city center is lovely, carefully platted beside the River Torrens and completely surrounded by a ring of spacious parkland.

I won't suggest a schedule here, since South Australia's attractions are in various directions from Adelaide and may not be practical to include in one itinerary without considerable time and/or money. Pick and choose spots that pique your interest.

Getting There

The major domestic carriers, Ansett and Australian airlines, serve Adelaide with nonstop daily flights to and from Sydney, Melbourne, Perth, and Alice Springs and regularly scheduled direct flights to and from Brisbane, Canberra, Darwin, the Gold Coast, and Queensland's Sunshine Coast. Air time from Sydney is about 1 hour, 50 minutes; from Perth, it's about 3 hours. South Australian time is 30 minutes behind Sydney, Melbourne, and Brisbane, but 1½ hours ahead of Western Australia. Several small carriers service local routes; most notable is Kendall Airlines, which flies an Adelaide-Coober Pedy-Ayers Rock service every Saturday morning.

You can rent a vehicle and drive directly from Melbourne, 747 km (464 mi.) via the Western and Dukes

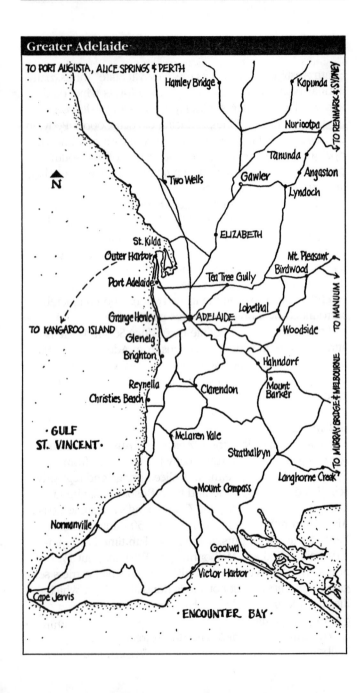

highways, or Sydney, 1,433 km (890 mi.) via the Mid Western and Stuart highways. Brisbane is 2,056 km (1,277 mi.) by the shortest route, Alice Springs is 1,697 km (1,054 mi.), and if you're really adventurous, Perth is 2,720 km (1,690 mi.) across the treacherous Nullarbor Plain. (Null arbor = "no vegetation.") Interstate buses travel these highways daily.

Rail service is also regular and efficient, with daily connections from Melbourne and Perth, six days a week from Sydney, and the famous "Ghan" weekly from Alice Springs.

Getting Around

You can rent a car at the airport or take the half-hourly Transit Regency coach into the city for A$3.50. Once you've arrived in Adelaide, the public transportation system—called the **State Transport Authority** (12A Grenfell Street, tel. 210-1000)—will take good care of you. Buses run north to Elizabeth, south to Reynella, and east through the many communities of the Adelaide Hills. Suburban trains operate over a wider area, while the city's only electric tram links downtown with the seaside suburb of Glenelg. The interconnecting services run from 6:00 a.m. to 11:30 p.m. Monday through Saturday, 9:00 a.m. to 10:30 p.m. Sunday. Fares start at A$1.20.

Adelaide Highlights

It makes sense for Adelaide visitors to focus their sight-seeing attentions on ▲▲**North Terrace**, the broad thoroughfare that demarcates the north end of downtown. On or near this street, you'll find the Adelaide Casino, Constitutional Museum, the Festival Centre, Government House, State Library, South Australian Museum, Art Gallery of South Australia, University of Adelaide, Ayers House, and the Botanic Gardens—all within a five-block stretch.

▲▲**The Festival Centre**, on King William Road within a diva's trill of North Terrace, is Adelaide's best-known building and the site of a major international arts festival in February and March of every even-numbered year (i.e., 1992, 1994). This performing arts complex contains a concert hall, three indoor theaters, and an open-air amphitheater. Guided tours, at A$3, are offered daily except Sunday, 9:30 a.m. to 4:45 p.m., though hours may be altered slightly by exhibitions. Book with the tours office (tel. 216-8713).

▲▲**The South Australian Museum** is one of Australia's best museums, particularly for anthropology and geology. Of special note are the Aboriginal artifacts and Australite meteorites, both said to be the world's largest collections of their types. Free tours at 2:15 and 3:00 p.m. Sunday.

▲**The Art Gallery of South Australia**, next door to the museum, has the requisite displays of Australian, English, and European paintings and decorative arts, plus a fine collection of Asian ceramics: Chinese, Annamese, and Thai. Admission is free.

▲▲**The Migration and Settlement Museum**, behind the State Library at 82 Kintore Avenue, recounts the struggle of Australian immigrants of the nineteenth and twentieth centuries and highlights the cultures of eight leading ethnic minorities of modern South Australia. Free admission.

▲**The Old Parliament House** museum of political history occupies the former South Australian Legislative Council chambers, built in 1855. A walking tour costs A$3; if you've got a spare hour and 40 minutes, the audio-visual presentation "Bound for South Australia" relates a full social and political history of this state.

▲**Ayers House**, 288 North Terrace, is a nineteenth-century mansion furnished in period style. Built in stages between 1846 and 1875, it was the residence of Sir Henry Ayers, premier of South Australia. Today, it contains two restaurants and the local headquarters of the National Trust. Closed Mondays; guided tours, A$3, are offered by appointment (tel. 223-1655).

▲**Tandanya Aboriginal Cultural Institute**, 253 Grenfell Street, fosters modern Aboriginal talents in visual and performing arts, and opens its museum to the public daily. Admission is A$4.

▲**The Zoological Gardens** on Frome Road has a superb collection of native birds plus many rare specimens bred in captivity. Admission is A$7.50.

▲**The South Australian Maritime Museum**, 119 Lipson Street, Port Adelaide, has an enormous collection of marine artifacts documenting the state's maritime history. Closed Thursday and Friday; admission is A$6.

▲**Glenelg** is Adelaide's most famous beach, a short trip from the city center by train. Captain John Windmarsh landed here and proclaimed the colony of South Australia in 1836; a replica of his boat, the *H.M.S. Buffalo*, contains restaurants and a museum (admission A$2.50). Down the shore is a major amusement center, Magic Mountain.

▲**Carrick Hill**, 590 Fullarton Road, Springfield, a circa-1939 Elizabethan-style manor house surrounded by 96 acres of gardens and bushland, contains a priceless private art collection of nineteenth- and twentieth-century oils, silver, pewter, and furniture.

▲▲▲**The Adelaide Hills** rise above the coastal plain 20 minutes' drive east of the city center. Their charm is in their views, bushland reserves, and numerous unique villages scattered through the gentle valleys. **Hahndorf**, 28 km (17 miles) from Adelaide, was founded in 1839 by German refugees and is still "sehr Deutsch"; many original stone buildings house hotels, restaurants, and artisans' studios. **Birdwood Mill National Motor Museum** at Birdwood has 300 vintage vehicles and other antiques in an old flour mill (admission A$6). **Cleland Conservation Park**, on the slopes of 2,333-foot Mount Lofty, is a great place for bushwalking and for viewing native wildlife.

South Australia Highlights

▲▲▲**The Barossa Valley** is the largest wine-producing district in Australia's major wine-producing state. Fifty separate wineries, most of them located in a stretch of 23 km (14 miles) along the Barossa Valley Highway between Lyndoch and Nuriootpa, open their cellar doors daily for tastings of their exquisite clarets and rieslings. The center of the region is Tanunda, a German town established in 1843 and the focus of the Barossa Valley Vintage Festival, held in April of every odd-numbered year (i.e., 1993, 1995).

▲▲**The Flinders Ranges** comprise a majestic set of sharp granite peaks and deep gorges 350 to 620 km (215 to 385 mi.) north of Adelaide. Within this wilderness are ancient Aboriginal sites, abandoned mining towns, geological oddities, two national parks (Flinders Ranges and Gammon), and the Wilpena Pound, an enormous natural amphitheater surrounded by steep cliffs.

▲▲▲**Coober Pedy** is one of the world's most unusual communities. Most of the 2,100 residents of this opal mining town, 943 km (586 mi.) northwest of Adelaide by road, live in underground "dugouts" (homes) to escape the blistering desert heat. (The town's name derives from an Aboriginal phrase, "kupa piti," meaning "white man's hole.") More than half the world's opals are mined at Coober Pedy. You can see demonstrations of opal cutting and polishing, or even get a budget bed, at the Umoona Mine; explore an underground display home and church, visit a museum, and shop for raw or cut opals. Coober Pedy is a good overnight stop between Adelaide and Alice Springs. Its distinctive **Desert Cave**, Hutchinson Street (tel. 086/72-5688), is billed as the world's first high-class underground hotel.

▲▲**Kangaroo Island**, Australia's third-largest offshore island, is best known for its plentiful wildlife. Some 150 km (90 mi.) long, it is connected to Adelaide by several flights a day (A$102 round-trip) and a daily ferry from

Cape Jervis (A$26 one way, leaving at 10:00 a.m., arriving at 11:30 a.m.). If you want to make it a day trip, tour prices begin at A$121. The main town, Kingscote, is a farming center, but the main visitor draw is **Flinders Chase National Park**, where kangaroos, koalas, emus, and other native species run wild. Divers enjoy exploring off-shore shipwrecks; fishing, bush-walking, and sunning on the beaches are also popular.

▲▲**The Murray River** is Australia's "Old Man River." Longer, at 1,609 miles, than most North American rivers (except the Mississippi, Yukon, and Missouri), it drains almost one-seventh of the Australian continent. Its final (and broadest) 400 miles cut through South Australia, emptying into Lake Alexandrina and Encounter Bay just south of Tailem Bend. You can cruise the river aboard a fully contained paddle-wheeler like the *Proud Mary*, which sails between Murray Bridge and Renmark on 5-day or overnight cruises (33 Pirie St., Adelaide; tel. 08/51-9472); or rent your own houseboat: contact the Lower Murray Regional Tourist Association, P.O. Box 344, Murray Bridge, SA 5253 (tel. 085/32-6660), for booking details.

Helpful Hints
Tourism South Australia has its main offices at 18 King William Street near North Terrace (tel. 212-1505). The agency operates a free information and booking service for hotels and tours throughout Adelaide and the state. It's open Monday through Friday 9:00 a.m. to 5:00 p.m., weekends and holidays 9:00 a.m. to 2:00 p.m.

PERTH AND WESTERN AUSTRALIA

Perth doesn't fit neatly into a 22-day itinerary merely
because of its isolation from the rest of Australia.
Adelaide, some 2,200 km (1,400 mi.) distant (by air), is
the nearest city with more than 25,000 people; and
Jakarta, Indonesia, is closer to Perth than is the Australian
national capital, Canberra.

For those with time, however, it's well worth a visit.
Perth, where 1.1 million of the 1.6 million Western
Australians live, is a lovely Mediterranean-style city nestled along the shores of the broad Swan River. Best
known in recent years as the temporary (1983-1987)
home of the America's Cup of yachting, Perth is the gateway to a vast and varied state that is larger than France.

Suggested 4-Day Schedule	
Day 1	Arrive in Perth. Enjoy a walking tour of the city, from London Court to Kings Park.
Day 2	Spend the day in Fremantle, an atmospheric European-style port town and the site of the 1987 America's Cup yacht races.
Day 3	Cruise the Swan River, passing the Royal Perth Yacht Club and continuing to Rottnest Island, where you can bicycle among the quokkas.
Day 4	Final sightseeing before an onward flight.

Getting There

Ansett, Australian, and Compass airlines have nonstop
daily flights to Perth from Adelaide, Melbourne, and
Sydney and regular direct flights from Brisbane, Cairns,
Mount Isa, Alice Springs, Darwin, and Port Hedland. Air
time from Sydney is about 4½ hours, from Adelaide
around 3 hours. (Perth time is 2 hours behind Sydney
and Melbourne, 1½ hours behind Adelaide and the
Northern Territory.) Think twice before driving across the
seemingly endless Western Australian desert to Perth.

Taking the train, however, is a wise alternative to flying. The "Indian-Pacific" takes 66 hours from Sydney, via Broken Hill, Adelaide, and Kalgoorlie, three times a week; the "Trans-Australian" runs 38 hours from Adelaide (with connections from Melbourne) twice a week.

Getting Around
Rent a car at the domestic airport, 11 km (7 mi.) from downtown, or the international terminal, 20 km (12½ mi.) away; take the Skybus coach to downtown Perth or major hotels for A$5; or catch a city bus. The public transportation system, called **Transperth** (125 St. George's Terrace, tel. 221-1211) operates buses and trains weekly from 6:00 a.m. to 11:00 p.m., with reduced services on weekends and holidays. Tickets good for a full day on all services cost A$4.60. Free buses circle the city at ten-minute intervals from 7:30 a.m. to 5:00 p.m. weekdays, 9:00 to 11:30 a.m. Saturdays.

Perth Sightseeing Highlights
▲▲▲A walk down **St. George's Terrace** offers a look at some of Perth's most historic buildings, dating from the 1850s, plus some unusual shopping arcades—notably **London Court**, reminiscent of a quaint Elizabethan-era alley.
▲▲**Kings Park** overlooks the west side of downtown. This 1,000-acre expanse, one of Australia's nicest city parks, contains a botanical garden, a restaurant, numerous picnic grounds, fountains, and memorials, and some grand views across Perth and the Swan River.
▲**The Western Australian Museum**, Francis at Beaufort streets, Northbridge (across the railroad tracks from downtown), is interesting for its natural antiquities—an 11-ton meteorite, for instance, and a 30-foot whale skeleton. It also has an Aboriginal gallery, wildlife displays, and the original 1856 Perth jail. Free admission.
▲**The Art Gallery of Western Australia**, adjacent to the museum on James Street at Beaufort, shares the Perth

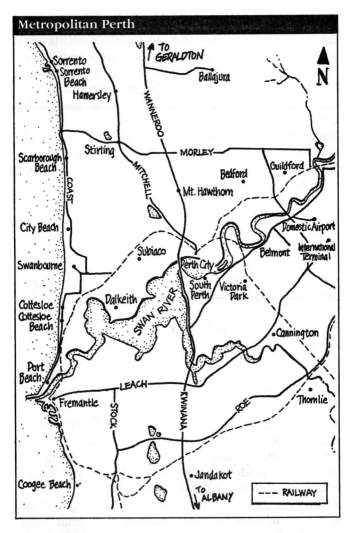

Metropolitan Perth

Cultural Centre with the Alexander Library. The A$10-million gallery has a superb permanent collection of Australian (especially W.A.) and foreign works, among them Cézanne, Monet, Picasso, Rembrandt, Renoir, van Gogh, and Whistler, plus a fine display of tribal art and regional crafts. Free admission.

▲▲▲**Cruises on the Swan River** leave from the Barrack Street Jetty at the foot of downtown. **Transperth** offers a 2:00 p.m. upriver cruise daily (returning at 4:45 p.m.) with an adult fare of A$10. **Captain Cook Cruises** has three-hour daily cruises priced at A$16.50, leaving at 10:00 a.m. and 1:45 p.m.; **Swan River Cruises** has 90-minute (A$9) and three-hour (A$14) departures at 9:30 p.m. daily. Your narrator will point out the Royal Perth Yacht Club—the holder of the America's Cup from 1983 to 1987—and the homes of many of the city's wealthier residents. You'll also see a great many sailboards and other water sports. With no major industry on the river, it is virtually without pollution.

▲▲▲**Beaches** in Perth are among the finest in Australia. Long strands of shimmering white sands extend from the Swan River mouth at North Fremantle for many miles north. Best known from south to north, are **North Cottesloe**, Prince Charles's personal favorite; **Swanbourne**, Perth's No. 1 nude beach; **City Beach**, a family beach with modern facilities; and **Scarborough**, site of the A$100 million Observation City resort hotel complex.

▲▲**Armadale**, a Perth suburb about 24 km (15 mi.) south of downtown, is the home of **Pioneer World**, a re-created working village of the late 1800s with various merchants and tradesmen, a police station, a fire station, a general store, a schoolhouse, a theater, and a stream for gold panning.

Fremantle Sightseeing Highlights
Western Australia's major port, settled in 1829, is situated at the mouth of the Swan River, just 19 km (12 mi.) downstream from Perth. At once more historic and more cosmopolitan than its "big brother," it features many nineteenth-century European-style buildings (more than 150 classified by the National Trust), an active and highly visible artisans' community, and of course its harbor and yachting marina. Fremantle is 35 minutes by Transperth

train from downtown Perth; the one-way fare is A$1.40.

▲▲**The Fremantle Museum and Arts Centre**, 1 Finnerty Street at Ord Street, is housed in a handsome stone building constructed in 1860 as a convict lunatic asylum. There are exhibits on the colonial history of Fremantle, the Swan River, and the Western Australian coast, plus a fine display of local ceramics, sculpture, textiles, paintings, and prints.

▲▲**The Western Australian Maritime Museum**, Cliff Street, exhibits artifacts of W.A.'s rich trading and whaling history. Its star attraction is the *Batavia*, a Dutch sailing vessel shipwrecked in 1629 and now being reassembled timber by timber in the museum.

▲**The America's Cup Museum**, 43 Swan Street, North Fremantle, has a collection of model yachts from the first America's Cup race through to the present day, including the 1987 series, when the swiftest 12-meter sailing ships in the world made their homes in Fremantle for several months.

▲▲**The Round House**, on Arthur Head at the west end of High Street, is the state's oldest surviving building. Constructed in 1831 as the Swan River Colony's original civil jail, it affords an excellent view across Fremantle and the harbor. Other convict-era structures include the grim-looking **Fremantle Gaol**, The Terrace (off Fairbairn Street), built by convicts between 1851 and 1859 and still used as a prison; and the **Warders' Quarters** on Henderson Street, stone terrace houses for prison guards and wardens.

▲**Fremantle Markets**, South Terrace and Henderson Street, are a great place to browse for an artsy bargain or indulge in a variety of ethnic foods. Open Friday through Sunday except holidays.

Rottnest Island

Perhaps the biggest surprise of many on this 5-by-11-km (3-by-7-mi.) island, 18 km (11 mi.) offshore from Fremantle, is that real estate developers haven't given it a new name. Its present monicker was provided by Dutch Commodore Willem de Vlamingh in 1696 when he mistook the native quokkas, miniature kangaroos, for rats. Developed in the 1830s as a convict farm colony, it was converted to minor resort status in 1917. The **Rottnest Museum**, housed in the 1857 grain-crushing mill, will tell you about the island's historic cottages and natural history. The **Underwater Explorer**, a semi-submersible submarine, offers cruises to look at shipwrecks, marine life, and reef formations. But the best way to see the island is to rent a bicycle from **Rottnest Bike Hire**, just behind the Hotel Rottnest and pay A$8 to pedal around for half a day. (There are no cars on the island.) Visit the salt lakes with their rich bird life, World War II gun emplacements, a lighthouse on the island's highest point, and impressive sandy beaches inviting you for a swim. You're almost sure to see the friendly little quokkas: the entire island is a wildlife sanctuary.

Get to Rottnest one of three ways. A **ferry** leaves Perth's Barracks Street Jetty daily at 9:00 a.m., stopping in Fremantle en route to Rottnest; return fare is A$35 from Perth, A$28 from Fremantle. **Boat Torque Cruises** operates A$32 shuttles as well as a full-day package excursion, leaving Perth daily at 9:00 a.m. (returning at 5:45 p.m.), including lunch at Rottnest and a two-hour minibus tour of the island for A$50. By air, it's a A$66.50 round-trip aboard **Rottnest Airbus** from the Perth Flight Centre at Perth airport, Redcliffe (tel. 478-1322). Several lodgings are available on the island. Check with the Rottnest Island Authority (tel. 292-5044).

Highlights of Western Australia

Western Australia is Australia's largest state, sprawling across 965,000 square miles from the tropical Kimberley to the forests and meadows of the Southwest. Most of it is foreboding desert and stark terrain suitable for miners and kangaroos. But there are numerous areas of tourist interest for those with time and inclination.

▲▲**The Southwest** is the state's most fertile region. Besides its orchards, vineyards, and cattle farms, there are surfing beaches and limestone caves along the west coast, forests of karri trees (300 feet high, 23 feet around) near Pemberton, the startling bluffs of the **Stirling Range National Park**, and the famous **Wave Rock** near Hyden. The largest towns are **Albany** (pop. 22,000), a beach town and agricultural center, and **Esperance** (pop. 7,000), gateway to the Archipelago of the Recherche, famous among divers. Australians flock to the Southwest in droves between August and November, when spring speckles the meadows and mountain slopes with 8,000 varieties of colorful wildflowers.

▲▲**The Goldfields** district focuses on **Kalgoorlie** (pop. 25,000), center of the state's gold mining industry, 597 km (371 mi.) east of Perth. Not quite a century ago, some 200,000 hopeful "diggers" worked this desert region seeking their fortunes. Kalgoorlie's wide streets and false-fronted hotels today are reminders of the gold rush era. Travelers visit the Hainault Tourist Mine to learn past and modern gold mining methods, both under and above ground. Brothels, not legal, are tolerated here. Most of the nearby towns built in the decade following the 1893 discovery of gold—like Gwalia, Broad Arrow, and Menzies—are now ghost towns. Alone among them, **Coolgardie** has been preserved as a living monument to the era, although its population has shrunk from 15,000 to 900. Don't miss the **Goldfields Museum**, open daily.

▲▲**The Midlands** include numerous fascinating attractions within a day's drive north and east of Perth. **The Pinnacles**, calcified spires of an ancient forest 30,000 years old, are in Nambung National Park. **New Norcia** is a fragment of medieval Spain, complete with a Benedictine monastery and an astounding museum and art gallery. **York** is the historical (1840s) center of the agriculturally rich Avon Valley.

▲**The North Coast** starts at **Geraldton** (pop. 21,000), a farming and lobster-fishing center 423 km (263 mi.) north of Perth. Many famous shipwrecks, including the 1629 *Batavia* disaster, occurred in the Abrolhos Isles offshore. A short distance north is the self-proclaimed **Principality of Hutt**, where Prince Leonard, a former farmer with his tongue firmly in cheek, even issues his own postage stamps. **Kalbarri National Park** features some spectacular gorges on the Murchison River. **Carnarvon** (pop. 5,000), 801 km (498 mi.) from Perth, is famous for its banana farms and prawning. **Port Hedland** (pop. 12,000), 1,547 km (978 mi.) from Perth on Highway 1, is the principal port for the Pilbara, Australia's major iron-ore region. At nearby Marble Bar, temperatures once exceeded 100 degrees F for five straight months.

▲▲**The Kimberley** is a remote, rugged region best seen during the cool, dry winter season (May to August). **Geikie Gorge**, on the Fitzroy River, and **Windjana Gorge**, on the Meda, are the most remarkable of several grandiose chasms in the King Leopold Ranges. **Tunnel Creek** has gouged a half-mile natural tunnel through limestone. The indented coastline is notable for its prolific crop of crocodiles! (Tourists beware: an American woman was gobbled alive in 1987.) **Broome** (pop. 4,000), 2,151 km (1,337 mi.) from Perth, is a former pearl-diving center that has shifted its economic base to cultured pearls. Its blend of Europeans and third-generation Japanese, Malays, and other Asians is unique in Australia. Northeast of the Kimberley, **Kununurra** (pop. 2,500), 3,140 km (1,951 mi.) from Perth, was founded in 1960 as a base for the massive Ord River Irrigation Scheme. Water sports and cruises are popular on Lake Argyle, W.A.'s biggest inland body of water. The world's largest diamond mine opened in the Bungle Bungle Range near here in 1985 after a major deposit was discovered; tours are available.

Helpful Hints
The **Western Australian Tourism Commission** has its offices at 722 Hay Street, Perth (tel. 09/322-2999). For everyday information and bookings, visit the **W.A. Tourist Centre** at Albert Facey House, Forrest Place at Wellington Street (tel. 483-3111). There's also a **Perth Convention Bureau**, 16 St. George's Terrace, 11th Floor (tel. 220-1737).

DARWIN AND THE "TOP END"

The main reason to go to Australia's "Top End"—the northern crown of the Northern Territory—is to visit Kakadu National Park. If you saw *Crocodile Dundee* and savored the fantastic wetland wilderness in which most of the Australian segment of the movie was filmed, you know just what Kakadu looks like.

Darwin, the gateway to Kakadu, is the hard-drinking capital of the Northern Territory. It has survived Japanese bombing in 1942 and a devastating cyclone in 1974 to become an interesting cosmopolitan city of 70,000.

Your schedule in the "Top End" should allow you a day in Darwin, as much time as you can make available in Kakadu, and possible side trips to Katherine Gorge and/or the Aboriginal communities on Bathurst and Melville islands. Keep in mind, though, that the oppressively humid wet season, from late November through March, is probably not a good time to visit.

Getting There

There are direct daily flights to Darwin from Adelaide, Alice Springs, Brisbane, Melbourne, Perth, and Sydney aboard Ansett, Ansett W.A., or Australian airlines, and additional direct flights (not daily) from Cairns, Mount Isa, and Port Hedland. Air time from Alice Springs is 1 hour, 50 minutes; from Sydney, 4½ hours; from Perth (with one stop), 4 hours. Ansett N.T. offers nonstop flights several times a week to and from Katherine, Tennant Creek, and Gove/Nhulunbuy in the Northern Territory. There are also international connections to Indonesia and Singapore.

There's no train service to Darwin, but you can travel overland by private car—a grueling effort, not recommended—or by express coach. No doubt the cheapest way to reach Darwin from major population centers is with an unlimited-mileage bus pass from Ansett, Pioneer, Greyhound, or Deluxe Coaches.

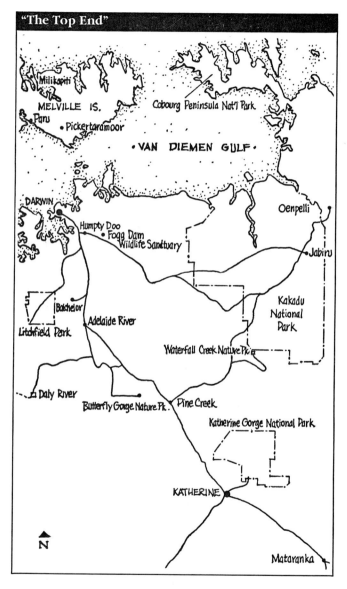

"The Top End"

Milikapiti

MELVILLE IS.

Paru • Pickertaramoor

Cobourg Peninsula Nat'l Park

• VAN DIEMEN GULF •

DARWIN

Humpty Doo

• Fogg Dam
Wildlife Sanctuary

Oenpelli

Jabiru

Batchelor

Adelaide River

Litchfield Park

Kakadu
National
Park

Waterfall Creek Nature Pk.

Daly River

Butterfly Gorge Nature Pk.

Pine Creek

Katherine Gorge National Park

KATHERINE

N

Mataranka

Getting Around

From Darwin airport, 8 km (5 mi.) from town, you can
rent a car, take a A$12 taxi ride, or hop on the airport

shuttle bus for a A$7 ride into downtown. Within the
city, public buses (tel. 81-2150) operate 6:00 a.m. to 11:00
p.m. Monday through Saturday, at a cost of A90 cents a
ride. You can also rent bicycles at **Darwin Bike Rentals**,
57 Mitchell Street near the Greyhound depot.

Top End Sightseeing Highlights

▲▲**Darwin**, founded in 1869, was named after naturalist
Charles Darwin by the captain of *H.M.S. Beagle*, who discovered the harbor 30 years earlier. The main sights
include the **Botanical Gardens**, established in 1891 and
now containing more than 400 species of tropical plants
on 85 acres; **Aquascene** at Doctor's Gully, where thousands of ocean fish come in at high tide daily for a free
feed of bread; the **N.T. Museum of Arts and Natural
Sciences**, notable for its primitive art and wildlife
exhibits; and the **Artillery Museum**, with reminders of
Darwin's World War II buffeting. If you're up here in
June, don't miss the **Beer Can Regatta**. Darwinites, who
consume an average of 60 gallons of beer per year for
every man, woman, and child, save up their empty cans
for 51 weeks to construct an imaginative flotilla that sets
sail on Darwin Harbour.

▲▲▲**Kakadu National Park** has been called the greatest wetland remaining on Planet Earth. Over 12,000
square miles in area, it comprises the floodplains of the
East, South, and West Alligator rivers and the Wildman
River, and the sudden cliffs of the Arnhem Land escarp-
ment with gorges, waterfalls, and 18,000-year-old
Aboriginal rock paintings. Join a safari for one to eight
days of bush-walking, camping, and cruising the rivers.
After joining one such expedition, my friend Elaine was
ecstatic. "Talk about a once-in-a-lifetime experience!" she
said. "I saw five crocodiles, water buffaloes, kangaroos,
dingos, bats, and more birds and insects than you can
imagine. The place was literally teeming with life." Book
a trip from Darwin with **Terra Safari Tours**, 1585 Strath
Road, Berrimah, NT (tel. 089/84-3470); or **Australian**

Kakadu Tours, P.O. Box 1397, Darwin (tel. 81-5144). Costs average around $150 a day, with lower prices for camping tours, higher prices for accommodated trips.

▲▲**Bathurst and Melville Islands**, traditional homes of the isolated Tiwi Aboriginal tribes, are situated 80 km (50 mi.) north of Darwin across the Clarence Strait. Tiwi pottery and woodcarvings, especially ceremonial grave poles, are unique. Contact **Tiwi Tours**, 27 Temira Crescent, Darwin (tel. 089/81-5144), to book a highly worthwhile half-day (A$135) or full-day (A$199) tour between March and October.

▲▲**Katherine Gorge National Park**, 31 km (19 mi.) from Katherine (pop. 4,500) and 388 km (241 mi.) southeast of Darwin, is best known for its boat trips between the sheer, 200-foot-high walls of the chasm. Two-hour cruises run four times daily most of the year for about A$25 adult fare.

Helpful Hints
You'll find the helpful **Northern Territory Government Tourist Bureau**, 31 Smith Street Mall (tel. 089/81-6611), open 8:45 a.m. to 5:00 p.m. Monday through Friday and 9:00 a.m. to 12:00 noon Saturday.

GREAT BARRIER REEF ISLANDS

If your visit to the Outer Reef (Day 17) whetted your
appetite for more time in the tropical sun, you'll be
pleased to know that there are hundreds of islands off the
coast of Queensland between the Gold Coast and Cape
Melville, spread across 1,300 km (800 mi.) of South Pacific
Ocean. Nearly two dozen of them have established resort
settlements.

Getting There

The main gateway towns are Bundaberg, Gladstone,
Rockhampton, Mackay, Proserpine, Townsville, Cardwell,
Tully, Cairns, and Cooktown, scattered up the coast north
of Brisbane. All are connected by highway; all but
Cooktown are linked via rail; all but Cardwell and Tully
have domestic airports of their own. Once you're reached
the gateway town, it's a relatively painless procedure to
get to the islands by boat (every resort has its own launch
service from nearby mainland harbors) or small plane.
Inquire locally for directions or check with the nearest
Queensland Government Travel Centre.

  The busiest gateway town is **Proserpine**, the takeoff
point for the Whitsunday Islands. Located 1,165 km (724
mi.) north of Brisbane and 650 km (404 mi.) south of
Cairns, it is served by nonstop flights from Brisbane,
Townsville, and Mackay several times a week and by
direct flights (with stops) from Sydney and Melbourne.
Coaches connect Proserpine with Shute Harbour, 22 km
(14 mi.) east, from which launches run several times daily
to the various resorts of the Whitsundays.

Island Highlights

Every Barrier Reef island has something a little different to
offer the visitor. Some are upscale, jet-set resorts, with all
manner of sports facilities and nightlife. Others are limited
to rustic cottages or youth hostel accommodations. You're
bound to find something to match your desires and price
range.

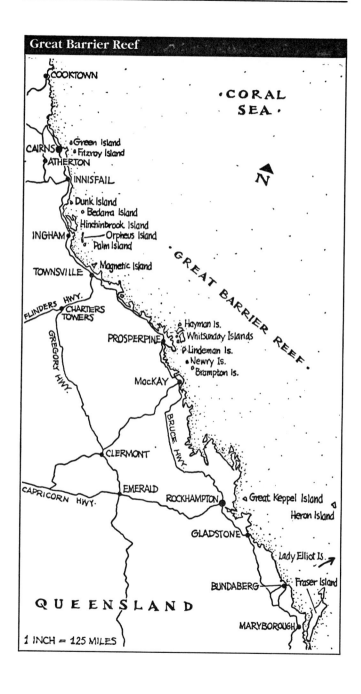

Great Barrier Reef

COOKTOWN

•CORAL
SEA•

Green Island
CAIRNS • Fitzroy Island
ATHERTON

INNISFAIL

N

Dunk Island
Bedarra Island
Hinchinbrook Island
INGHAM Orpheus Island
Palm Island

Magnetic Island
TOWNSVILLE

GREAT

FLINDERS HWY.
CHARTERS
TOWERS

BARRIER

GREGORY HWY.

Hayman Is.
PROSPERPINE Whitsunday Islands
Lindeman Is.
Newry Is.
Brampton Is.

REEF.

MacKAY

BRUCE HWY.

CLERMONT

CAPRICORN HWY. EMERALD
ROCKHAMPTON Great Keppel Island
Heron Island

GLADSTONE

Lady Elliot Is.

BUNDABERG Fraser Island

QUEENSLAND

MARYBOROUGH

1 INCH = 125 MILES

The following listing singles out major resort islands, starting in the south and moving north.

Lady Elliot Island is the southernmost coral cay on the reef. Visitors come to this tiny but high-priced isle to enjoy the marine life with tank, snorkel, or on foot at low tide. Full-board lodging costs A$240 in scattered cabins or safari tents. There's no launch service; charter aircraft from Bundaberg charge A$170 round-trip.

Heron Island is famous worldwide for its outstanding scuba diving and snorkeling. Just 42 acres in area, this unspoiled cay is surrounded by over 9 square miles of coral reef. The Barrier Reef Divers Festival is held here every November; the rest of the year, you can get excellent diving instruction and equipment. In addition to the reef life, you can see green sea turtles and migratory mutton birds nest here (the island is a national park) and lay their eggs in spring and summer. Launches leave Gladstone daily except Thursday at 8:00 a.m., arriving at Heron Island (a distance of 72 km, or 45 mi.) 2½ hours later, for A$130 round-trip. Or you can take a helicopter for A$280 round-trip.

Great Keppel Island is as frantic as Heron and Lady Elliot are serene. The largest of 27 mostly undeveloped islands in the Keppel Group, 13 km (8 mi.) east of Yeppoon, near Rockhampton, it is heavily geared toward singles in their 20s. At the main resort, activities are scheduled every minute of the day and night, from water sports to disco dancing (there's a resident rock band), tennis and golf to squash and cricket. The resort is owned by Australian Airlines, which offers weekly packages. To get to Great Keppel, take a coach from Rockhampton to Rosslyn Bay (near Yeppoon), then pay A$22-$27 round-trip for the hydrofoil. There are also several 25-minute flights daily from Rockhampton.

Brampton Island, 32 km (20 mi.) north of Mackay, is a national park and wildlife sanctuary. The mountainous, 1,100-acre island is cloaked in tropical forest and surrounded by white sand beaches and coral reefs. It's great for bushwalking among semi-tame kangaroos and color-ful lorikeets. At Brampton Island Resort, an Australian Airlines hotel, activities include all manner of water sports, tennis and golf, and a disco for nightlife. Lodging is A$800 per person, weekly. Launch service operates daily from Mackay at 9:00 a.m. The cruise takes an hour, and the cost is A$40 round-trip. If you prefer to fly, Australian Regional Airlines makes the short hop from Mackay.

Newry Island, a hilly, wooded national park of just 110 acres, is one of the least known (and most untouristy) of all the isles off the Queensland coast. Koalas and echidnas are native to the island, a good place for walking and swimming. A small resort accommodates 25 guests; camping is also available. A launch service operates from Victor Creek, 56 km (35 mi.) north of Mackay, at 11:00 a.m. every Wednesday, Saturday, and Sunday. It takes 15 minutes; the fare is A$10.

Lindeman Island is on the southern fringe of the Whitsunday Group, 74 islands discovered and named by Captain Cook in 1770. Lindeman was the first of the Barrier Reef resorts, established in 1929. Walking trails climb the hills of this rocky, 2,000-acre isle. There are organized activities for kids of all ages. Club Med bought the island in 1989 and has opened a new A$300-a-night (full-board) resort.

Hamilton Island is the luxurious, world-class resort center of the Whitsundays. The A$200 million hotel complex features five restaurants and a French bakery, seven bars (including one of the swim-up variety in Australia's largest freshwater pool), an indoor sports complex, a shopping center with four boutiques, a 200-acre fauna park, a 400-boat marina, sportfishing charters and scuba-diving instruction, and a "floating hotel," the Coral Cat, hovering above the reef. The 1,200-acre island is quite hilly, but there's enough flat ground for Queensland's only island airport where large jets can land. Ansett flies nonstop daily from Cairns and several times weekly from

Brisbane, Sydney, and Melbourne. A 45-minute launch service runs twice daily (9:00 a.m. and 4:45 p.m.) from Shute Harbour for a round-trip fare of A$30.

Long Island has two very different resort communities about 2 km apart. The Island Resort competes for the 18- to 35-year-old singles clientele of Great Keppel Island with nonstop water sports by day, disco dancing by night. Budget travelers, meanwhile, enjoy Palm Bay Resort, cook their own food (there's a small grocery), and enjoy bushwalking and snorkeling. Long Island is a lush national park 11 km (7 mi.) long, no more than 1½ km wide, and everywhere mountainous. Launches run four times daily (9:00 a.m. to 4:45 p.m.) from Shute Harbour, 8 km (5 mi.) northwest. The roundtrip fare is A$20 to Palm Bay.

South Molle Island is a 1,000-acre island of steep bush-covered hills and coral-fringed bays in the heart of the Whitsunday Passage. A national park, it is criss-crossed by walking tracks and inhabited by brightly col-ored lorikeets. The medium-sized resort offers water sports, fishing, a gymnasium, golf, and tennis. It is served by restaurants, bars, and other facilities. Launch service from Shute Harbour (daily at 9:00 a.m., 1:00 and 5:00 p.m.) costs A$25 round-trip.

Daydream Island is tiny, just three-fourths of a mile long and barely 500 meters (547 yards) wide. Social life on this speck of paradise, clutched by white coral beach-es and lazy coconut palms, focuses on the resort's huge lagoon-style swimming pool with its bar on a central island (no "dry" martinis here). There are the usual vari-ety of water and other sports and a disco for night. The island is served twice daily (9:00 a.m. and 5:00 p.m.) by launch from Shute Harbour, 5 km (3 mi.) distant, for A$25 round-trip.

Hayman Island, one of the oldest of the reef resorts (it dates from the 1950s), was reincarnated in 1986 as a five-star resort after a A$100 million renovation by Ansett. It's a universally appealing island with 1,000 acres of rugged mountain scenery, a wide fringe of reef, palm-shaded beaches, and dozens of species of birds and butterflies. The Ansett International Hotel has five restaurants, a library, a lively entertainment center, and fine water sports facilities. Rooms start at A$250 a night, and there's no launch service: Get there by helicopter from Proserpine or direct by Turbo Beaver from Airlie Beach (near Shute Harbour) or Townsville.

Magnetic Island is almost a suburb of Townsville. Just 13 km (8 mi.) north of Queensland's third-largest city, it attracts hundreds or even thousands of day-trippers. But it's big enough—20 square miles—that the throngs are easily escaped. Another mountainous national park island, it has fine bushwalking, a fernery and an aquarium, bird and koala sanctuaries, two dozen sandy beaches, and a motor road linking several resort villages along the eastern shore. (The island even has its own bus service.) You can rent bicycles or mopeds at Picnic Bay, where the ferry arrives 8 to 12 times daily from Townsville (35 minutes, A$12 round-trip). The island contains at least a half-dozen official and unofficial youth hostels, numerous holiday flats, and economy-priced hotels in Picnic Bay and Arcadia. Australian Airlines' Alma Dean Beach Resort midway up the east coast is a top resort.

Orpheus Island is one of the more secluded of the reef resorts, 80 km (50 mi.) northwest of Townsville and 24 km (15 mi.) east of Lucinda, near Ingham. Eleven km (7 mi.) long, not quite a mile wide, and fringed with reef, the forested island—volcanic in origin—is a national park rich in birdlife and turtle nesting grounds. There's no regular launch service, but seaplanes or helicopters operate daily from Townsville.

Hinchinbrook Island is the world's largest island national park, a 144-square-mile Tahitian landscape of lush rain forest, mist-shrouded mountains (up to 3,400 feet high), spectacular waterfalls, rocky caves, sandy beaches (on the east coast), and rich wildlife. A narrow channel separates it from the mainland east of Cardwell, about halfway between Townsville and Cairns. Launches leave Cardwell daily except Monday at 9:00 a.m., with a fare of A$40 round-trip.

Bedarra Island is a tiny and exclusive resort island. One mile long and a half-mile wide, four miles off the coast near Tully, it is densely forested and ringed by white sandy beaches. The new Bedarra Bay Resort consists of 24 elaborate guest bungalows set in a tropical garden along the ocean. There's no organized entertainment of any type—nothing but "intimate, casual and elegant" relaxation, as promoters put it. No one under 15 is allowed. Rates *start* at A$400 per person, per day.

Dunk Island is another unspoiled gem with a remarkably rich fauna and flora. Lush jungle caresses the slopes of 900-foot Mount Koo-tal-oo, providing a home for some 150 species of birds, plus dozens of beetles and butterflies, lizards and snakes, bats and echidnas. The island is only 520 acres in size, but it somehow seems larger. The sophisticated over-30 set likes its Great Barrier Reef Hotel, which offers all the sports of other island resorts plus horseback riding, skeet shooting, and nature activities. Get there on a launch from Clump Point, 5 km (3 miles) west, for A$20 return; water taxi from South Mission Beach; or a flight with Australian Airlines (the resort owner) daily from Townsville and several times a week from Cairns.

Green Island, just off Cairns, is a mere 32 acres in size, and nowhere more than 10 feet in elevation. It's cloaked in lush palms, figs, and other rain forest vegetation, has a beautiful white sand beach, and is reserved as a marine national park. Offshore snorkeling is excellent. A small resort on the island has recently been refurbished; it has lots to offer, including an underwater observatory and a marineland (with a 20-foot Guinness-class crocodile). Cruise boats make the 27-km (17-mi.) passage in 90 minutes for A$20 round-trip; luxury catamarans cover the distance in 40 minutes twice daily for A$28 round-trip, leaving Cairns at 8:30 and 10:30 a.m.

Fitzroy Island is ideal for travelers seeking a bit of isolation. The mountainous 750-acre island is shrouded in tropical rain forest and fringed by rugged coral beaches. There's an excellent reef 150 feet offshore for snorkeling and diving. Canoeing, paddle skiing, and bushwalking are other popular sports. Fitzroy Island Resort on Welcome Bay caters to budget travelers with hostel-style rooms (with communal kitchens) and guest villas. There's also a licensed restaurant. The island is 3½ miles off the coast, 16 miles southeast of Cairns. A catamaran leaves Cairns daily for Fitzroy at 9:00 a.m., returning at 1:30 p.m., for A$15 round-trip.

Lizard Island is the northernmost of the Barrier Reef resort islands, 95 km (59 mi.) northeast of Cooktown. Situated close to the magnificent outer reef, this 4-square-mile island has great beaches, fine snorkeling, and some of the world's finest big-game fishing within easy cast. Lizard Island Lodge is an exclusive resort overlooking a coral lagoon. Flights to Lizard Island run about A$140—each way—from Cairns.

Helpful Hints
Queensland Government Travel Centres are situated in three towns between Brisbane and Cairns: Rockhampton (119 East St. tel. 079/27-8611); Mackay (River St., tel. 079/57-2292); and Townsville (303 Flinders Mall, tel. 077/71-3077). The QGTC's main office is at 196 Adelaide Street, Brisbane, QLD 4000 (tel. 07/833-5255). Most of the reef resorts have postal service and shops; many also have banking facilities and resident medical practitioners.

Yes, Australians do speak English, but it often seems to be a different English language than most Americans are used to hearing. For starters, the dialect is a bit odd, with the long A sounding more like an I and the R, except at the beginning of a word, often dropped altogether. Once you begin to become accustomed to that, you find that there's a whole new vocabulary you never learned in school. The following list is an attempt to make your understanding a bit easier.

"Strine," by the way, was one foreigner's attempt to transliterate the word "Australian" as it is sometimes pronounced.

amber   beer
arvo   afternoon

back of beyond   the outback
back of Bourke   way out in the outback
banana bender   native Queenslander
barbie   barbecue
barrack   cheer the team to victory
beet root   red beet (always in hamburgers and salads)
belt up   shut up
bent   drunk or stoned
bickie (or biscuit)   cookie
bike   promiscuous woman
billabong   water hole in an intermittent river
billy   tin pot used to boil water for tea
biro   ballpoint pen
bitser   mongrel dog ("bitsa this, bitsa that")
bitumen   surfaced road
bloke   guy
bloody   a universal expletive
bloody oath   I agree! Damn right!
blotto   very drunk
blowfly   the Australian national pest
blue   fight

bludger　human parasite, lazy person
bo peep　quick look
bonnet　hood (of a vehicle)
bonzer　wonderful
boomer　very large; especially, a large kangaroo
boot　trunk (of a vehicle)
bottle shop　liquor store
bowser　gas pump; also, tanker truck
brekkie　breakfast
brolly　umbrella
brumby　wild horse
Buckley's chance　a snowball's chance in hell
bugger-all　nothing, as in "bugger-all money"
buggered　exhausted; also lewd meanings
Bullamakanka　beyond the back of Bourke
bull dust　fine, powdery dust on outback roads
bush　anything outside a town or city
bushranger　nineteenth-century outlaw
bushwalking　hiking
busker　street performer

caravan　trailer
chemist　pharmacist
chin wag　conversation
chock-a-block　100% full
chook　chicken
coach　tour bus or long-distance bus
cobber　mate
come a gutser　make a bad mistake
come the raw prawn　be deceitful
coolabah　a type of eucalyptus tree
corroboree　Aboriginal festival
cracker　biscuit
crook　sick, broken, or no good
cuppa　cup of tea (or coffee)
cut lunch　sandwiches

daks　trousers

damper   unleavened bread (bush tucker)
dijeridu (or didgeridoo)   Aboriginal musical
   instrument; it drones
digger   originally a gold miner; later a soldier; now,
   often, any Australian
dinkie die   fair dinkum
dinkum   honest, genuine
do your block   lose your temper
dob in   inform on, betray
drongo   born loser, ne'er-do-well
dunny   outhouse

ear bash   talk too much
entree   appetizer (not the main course)
Enzed   New Zealand
esky   portable cooler
evo   evening

fag   cigarette
fair dinkum   the complete, honest truth
fancy dress   masquerade costume
flake   shark meat (used in fish and chips)
flaming   another all-purpose expletive
flat   apartment
flog   sell, vend
footie   Australian football
footpath   sidewalk

g'day   universal greeting
galah   rose-colored cockatoo; also, a fool
get off your bike   become angry
give it a burl   give it a try
give it the flick   get rid of it
going troppo   moving to the far north
good on ya   "Way to go"
grazier   livestock rancher with large holdings
greengrocer   vegetable and fruit dealer
greenies   environmentalists
hang a Louie   do a left turn

hang a Roscoe   do a right turn
happy as Larry   fully content
hard case   enjoyable person to be around
have a bash   give a try
have on   accept a challenge; also, pull one's leg
hire   rent
holiday   vacation
hump   root; also, to carry (as a swag)

jackeroo   apprentice cowboy
jam   jelly
jilleroo   apprentice cowgirl
jumbuck   sheep
jumper   sweater

kip   bed
Kiwi   New Zealander
knackered   exhausted

Lamington   a cake with coconut-chocolate icing
larrikin   rabble rouser, hoodlum
lift   elevator
light globe   light bulb
lob in   arrive
lollies   candy
lolly water   soda pop

mate   close friend (not spouse)
matilda   belongings carried in a swag
middy   medium-sized glass of beer
milk bar   corner grocery
Moreton Bay bug   a small yabbie
mozzie   mosquito
mug   gullible person
mum   mom, or mother
muso   musician

napkin   baby's diaper
natter   gossip

Never Never   desert land, inhabited by Aboriginals
nick   steal
no worries   she'll be right
not in the race   out of luck

Ocker   stereotypical Aussie loudmouth
offsider   assistant; sometimes, spouse
on the turps   off the wagon
Oz   Australia

packet   envelope, usually containing paycheck
pavement   sidewalk
pavlova   traditional Aussie meringue dessert
penguin   nun
perve   scope out an attractive woman or man
peter   cash register
pinch   arrest
point the bone   hex (an Aboriginal superstition)
poker machine   slot machine
Pom   Englishman
pony   small glass of beer
postie   mail delivery person
pot   A victorian middy
power point   light socket
prang   crash or dent

queue   waiting line

rage   party
randy   sexually excited (horny)
rapt   enthralled
rave   animated conversation
return fare   round-trip fare
ridgy-didge   original, genuine
ripper   great!
roo   kangaroo
roos in his paddock   bats in his belfry
root   sexual intercourse; does not mean cheering for a
    team!

sandshoes   sneakers
schooner   large glass of beer
sea wasp   jellyfish with highly potent venom
sealed   paved (as a road)
Seppo   American (from rhyming slang: Yank = septic
   tank = Seppo)
serviette   table napkin
shandy   a beer-and-lemonade drink
sheila   young woman; "broad"
she'll be right   everything will be OK (also "she's
   jake," "she's sweet," "she'll be apples")
shoot through   leave suddenly
shop assistant   sales clerk
shout   buy a round of drinks
silk shirt on a pig   something wasted
silver beet   spinach
silvertail   member of high society
skite   brag, boast
sly grogger   after-hours drinking establishment
smoke-o   tea break
snag   sausage
solicitor   attorney
spit the dummy   have a fit, throw a tantrum;
   sometimes, give up or quit
sprog   baby
spunky   sexy-looking
station   large farm or ranch in the outback
stickybeak   busybody
stone   14 pounds (weight)
strewth!   It's the truth!
strides   trousers
swag   small bundle of personal belongings
swagman   hobo
Sydney or the bush   all or nothing

ta   Thanks!
TAB   "bettin' shop": Totalisator Agency Board
takeaway bar   fast-food restaurant
tall poppy   overachiever

taxi rank   cab stand
Tazzie   Tasmania
tinny   can of beer
togs (or cozzie)   swimsuit, "bathing costume"
too right   without question
torch   flashlight
track   outback road
tram   streetcar
trendy   akin to yuppie
tube   can of beer
tucker   food
two-pot screamer   person unable to hold his beer

uni (or varsity)   university
up a gum tree   in a dilemma
ute   utility truck; pickup truck

Vegemite   a strong-tasting brown-yeast sandwich
    spread, *very* Australian

walkabout   traveling on foot for a long way without a
    specific destination
walloper   policeman
waltz matilda   carry a swag
wanker   unproductive person, fool
welsh   fail to repay one's debts
wharfie   longshoreman
whinge   complain
white (coffee or tea)   served with milk or cream
witchety grubs   sweet worms, cooked in sauce
wowser   killjoy

yabber   chatter
yabbie   crawdad (small lobster)
yakka   work
Yank   American
Yank tank   large American automobile

Other Books from John Muir Publications

Asia Through the Back Door, 4th ed., 400 pp. $16.95 (available 7/93)

Belize: A Natural Destination, 336 pp. $16.95

Costa Rica: A Natural Destination, 2nd ed., 310 pp. $16.95

Elderhostels: The Students' Choice, 2nd ed., 304 pp. $15.95

Environmental Vacations: Volunteer Projects to Save the Planet, 2nd ed., 248 pp. $16.95

Europe 101: History & Art for the Traveler, 4th ed., 350 pp. $15.95

Europe Through the Back Door, 11th ed., 432 pp. $17.95

Europe Through the Back Door Phrase Book: French, 160 pp. $4.95

Europe Through the Back Door Phrase Book: German, 160 pp. $4.95

Europe Through the Back Door Phrase Book: Italian, 168 pp. $4.95

Europe Through the Back Door Phrase Book: Spanish & Portuguese, 288 pp. $4.95

A Foreign Visitor's Guide to America, 224 pp. $12.95

Great Cities of Eastern Europe, 256 pp. $16.95

Guatemala: A Natural Destination, 336 pp. $16.95

Indian America: A Traveler's Companion, 4th ed., 448 pp. $17.95 (available 7/93)

Interior Furnishings Southwest, 256 pp. $19.95

Mona Winks: Self-Guided Tours of Europe's Top Museums, 2nd ed., 448 pp. $16.95

Opera! The Guide to Western Europe's Great Houses, 296 pp. $18.95

Paintbrushes and Pistols: How the Taos Artists Sold the West, 288 pp. $17.95

The People's Guide to Mexico, 9th ed., 608 pp. $18.95

Ranch Vacations: The Complete Guide to Guest and Resort, Fly-Fishing, and Cross-Country Skiing Ranches, 2nd ed., 396 pp. $18.95

The Shopper's Guide to Art and Crafts in the Hawaiian Islands, 272 pp. $13.95

The Shopper's Guide to Mexico, 224 pp. $9.95

Understanding Europeans, 272 pp. $14.95

Undiscovered Islands of the Caribbean, 3rd ed., 288 pp. $14.95

Undiscovered Islands of the Mediterranean, 2nd ed., 224 pp. $13.95

Undiscovered Islands of the U.S. and Canadian West Coast, 288 pp. $12.95

Unique Colorado, 112 pp. $10.95 (available 6/93)
Unique Florida, 112 pp. $10.95 (available 7/93)
Unique New Mexico, 112 pp. $10.95 (available 6/93)
A Viewer's Guide to Art: A Glossary of Gods, People, and Creatures, 144 pp. $10.95
The Visitor's Guide to the Birds of the Eastern National Parks: United States and Canada, 410 pp. $15.95

2 to 22 Days Series

Each title offers 22 flexible daily itineraries useful for planning vacations of any length. Aside from valuable general information, included are "must see" attractions *and* hidden "jewels."

2 to 22 Days in the American Southwest, 1993 ed., 176 pp. $10.95

2 to 22 Days in Asia, 1993 ed., 176 pp. $9.95

2 to 22 Days in Australia, 1993 ed., 192 pp. $9.95

2 to 22 Days in California, 1993 ed., 192 pp. $9.95

2 to 22 Days in Europe, 1993 ed., 288 pp. $13.95

2 to 22 Days in Florida, 1993 ed., 192 pp. $10.95

2 to 22 Days in France, 1993 ed., 192 pp. $10.95

2 to 22 Days in Germany, Austria, & Switzerland, 1993 ed., 224 pp. $10.95

2 to 22 Days in Great Britain, 1993 ed., 192 pp. $10.95

2 to 22 Days Around the Great Lakes, 1993 ed., 192 pp. $10.95

2 to 22 Days in Hawaii, 1993 ed., 192 pp. $9.95

2 to 22 Days in Italy, 208 pp. $10.95

2 to 22 Days in New England, 1993 ed., 192 pp. $10.95

2 to 22 Days in New Zealand, 1993 ed., 192 pp. $9.95

2 to 22 Days in Norway, Sweden, & Denmark, 1993 ed., 192 pp. $10.95

2 to 22 Days in the Pacific Northwest, 1993 ed., 192 pp. $10.95

2 to 22 Days in the Rockies, 1993 ed., 192 pp. $10.95

2 to 22 Days in Spain & Portugal, 192 pp. $10.95

2 to 22 Days in Texas, 1993 ed., 192 pp. $9.95

2 to 22 Days in Thailand, 1993 ed., 180 pp. $9.95

22 Days (or More) Around the World, 1993 ed., 264 pp. $12.95

Automotive Titles

How to Keep Your VW Alive, 15th ed., 464 pp. $21.95
How to Keep Your Subaru Alive 480 pp. $21.95
How to Keep Your Toyota Pickup Alive 392 pp. $21.95
How to Keep Your Datsun/Nissan Alive 544 pp. $21.95
The Greaseless Guide to Car Care Confidence, 224 pp. $14.95
Off-Road Emergency Repair & Survival, 160 pp. $9.95

TITLES FOR YOUNG READERS AGES 8 AND UP

"Kidding Around" Travel Guides for Young Readers

All the "Kidding Around" Travel guides are 64 pages and $9.95 paper, except for **Kidding Around Spain** and **Kidding Around the National Parks of the Southwest**, which are 108 pages and $12.95 paper.

Kidding Around Atlanta
Kidding Around Boston, 2nd ed.
Kidding Around Chicago, 2nd ed.
Kidding Around the Hawaiian Islands
Kidding Around London
Kidding Around Los Angeles
Kidding Around the National Parks of the Southwest
Kidding Around New York City, 2nd ed.
Kidding Around Paris
Kidding Around Philadelphia
Kidding Around San Diego
Kidding Around San Francisco
Kidding Around Santa Fe
Kidding Around Seattle
Kidding Around Spain
Kidding Around Washington, D.C., 2nd ed.

"Extremely Weird" Series for Young Readers.

Written by Sarah Lovett, each is 48 pages and $9.95 paper.

Extremely Weird Bats
Extremely Weird Birds
Extremely Weird Endangered Species
Extremely Weird Fishes
Extremely Weird Frogs
Extremely Weird Insects
Extremely Weird Mammals (available 8/93)
Extremely Weird Micro Monsters (available 8/93)
Extremely Weird Primates
Extremely Weird Reptiles
Extremely Weird Sea Creatures
Extremely Weird Snakes (available 8/93)
Extremely Weird Spiders

"Masters of Motion" Series for Young Readers.

Each title is 48 pages and $9.95 paper.

How to Drive an Indy Race Car
How to Fly a 747
How to Fly the Space Shuttle

"X-ray Vision" Series for Young Readers.

Each title is 48 pages and $9.95 paper.

Looking Inside Cartoon Animation
Looking Inside Sports Aerodynamics

Looking Inside the Brain
Looking Inside Sunken Treasure
Looking Inside Telescopes and the Night Sky

Multicultural Titles for Young Readers
Native Artists of North America, 48 pp. $14.95 hardcover
The Indian Way: Learning to Communicate with Mother Earth, 114 pp. $9.95
The Kids' Environment Book: What's Awry and Why, 192 pp. $13.95
Kids Explore America's African-American Heritage, 112 pp. $8.95
Kids Explore America's Hispanic Heritage, 112 pp. $7.95

Environmental Titles for Young Readers
Rads, Ergs, and Cheeseburgers: The Kids' Guide to Energy and the Environment, 108 pp. $12.95
Habitats: Where the Wild Things Live, 48 pp. $9.95
The Kids' Environment Book: What's Awry and Why, 192 pp. $13.95

Ordering Information
Please check your local bookstore for our books, or call 1-800-888-7504 to order direct from us. All orders are shipped via UPS; see chart below to calculate your shipping charge to U.S. destinations. **No P.O. Boxes please; we must have a street address to ensure delivery.** If the book you request is not available, we will hold your check until we can ship it. Foreign orders will be shipped surface rate unless otherwise requested; please enclose $3.00 for the first item and $1.00 for each additional item.

For U.S. Orders Totaling	Add
Up to $15.00	$4.25
$15.01 to $45.00	$5.25
$45.01 to $75.00	$6.25
$75.01 or more	$7.25

Methods of Payment
Check, money order, American Express, MasterCard, or Visa. We cannot be responsible for cash sent through the mail. For credit card orders, include your card number, expiration date, and your signature, or call (800) 888-7504. American Express card orders can be shipped only to billing address of cardholder. Sorry, no C.O.D.'s. Residents of sunny New Mexico, add 6.125% tax to total.

Address all orders and inquiries to:
John Muir Publications
P.O. Box 613
Santa Fe, NM 87504
(505) 982-4078
(800) 888-7504